Contents

HANDS-ON HISTORY

TECHNOLOGY

BRING THE PAST ALIVE WITH
20 GREAT HISTORY PROJECTS

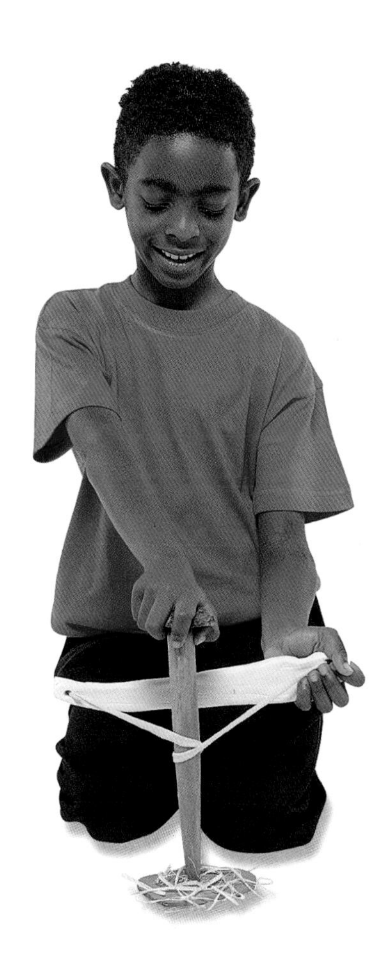

Consulting editors Rachel Halstead
and Struan Reid

This edition is published by Southwater

Southwater is an imprint of Anness Publishing Ltd
Hermes House, 88–89 Blackfriars Road, London SE1 8HA
tel. 020 7401 2077; fax 020 7633 9499
www.southwaterbooks.com; info@anness.com

UK agent: The Manning Partnership Ltd,
6 The Old Dairy, Melcombe Road, Bath BA2 3LR
tel. 01225 478 444; fax 01225 478 440
sales@manning-partnership.co.uk

UK distributor: Grantham Book Services Ltd,
Isaac Newton Way, Alma Park Industrial Estate
Grantham, Lincs NG31 9SD
tel. 01476 541080; fax 01476 541061
orders@gbs.tbs-ltd.co.uk

North American agent/distributor: National Book Network
4501 Forbes Boulevard, Suite 200, Lanham, MD 20706
tel. 301 459 3366; fax 301 429 5746; www.nbnbooks.com

Australian agent/distributor: Pan Macmillan Australia
Level 18, St Martins Tower, 31 Market St, Sydney
NSW 2000; tel. 1300 135 113; fax 1300 135 103
customer.service@macmillan.com.au

A CIP catalogue record for this book is available from the British Library.

Publisher: Joanna Lorenz
Managing Editor: Linda Fraser
Editors: Leon Gray, Sarah Uttridge
Designer: Sandra Marques/Axis Design Editions Ltd
Jacket Design: Dean Price
Photographers: Paul Bricknell and John Freeman
Illustrators: Rob Ashby, Julian Baker, Andy Beckett, Mark Beesley, Mark Bergin, Richard Berridge, Peter Bull Art Studio, Vanessa Card, Stuart Carter, Rob Chapman, James Field, Wayne Ford, Chris Forsey, Mike Foster, Terry Gabbey, Roger Gorringe, Jeremy Gower, Peter Gregory, Stephen Gyapay, Ron Hayward, Gary Hincks, Sally Holmes, Richard Hook, Rob Jakeway, John James, Kuo Chen Kang, Aziz Khan, Stuart Lafford, Ch'en Ling, Steve Lings, Kevin Maddison, Janos Marffy, Shane Marsh, Rob McCaig, Chris Odgers, Alex Pang, Helen Parsley, Terry Riley, Andrew Robinson, Chris Rothero, Eric Rowe, Martin Sanders, Peter Sarson, Mike Saunders, Rob Sheffield, Don Simpson, Guy Smith, Donato Spedaliere, Nick Spender, Clive Spong, Stuart Squires, Roger Stewart, Sue Stitt, Ken Stott, Steve Sweet, Mike Taylor, Alisa Tingley, Catherine Ward, Shane Watson, Ross Watton, Alison Winfield, John Whetton, Mike White, Stuart Wilkinson, John Woodcock
Stylists: Jane Coney, Konika Shakar, Thomasina Smith, Melanie Williams

Previously published as part of a larger compendium, *120 Great History Projects*

Picture credit: The Art Archive:/Oriental Art Museum Genoa/Dagli Orti, 23tr

10 9 8 7 6 5 4 3 2 1

Ancient Egyptian agriculture on the bank of the River Nile

Science and Technology

Discovery, invention and progress went hand-in-hand with civilization. Systems of writing, weights and measures, currency and communication were vital to running a successful empire. Transport and travel were the key to trade and expansion of territory. The projects in this section provide an insight into the developing technologies, such as transport and warfare, that gave people the edge over their neighbours.

Inventions and Learning

Humans have striven to understand the world around them ever since they first walked on the Earth some 30,000 years ago. The earliest people lived by hunting animals and gathering fruit. Their inventions were simple tools and weapons. Farming and permanent settlements, and the subsequent development of towns and cities, made life much more complicated. This, together with increased wealth, prompted some remarkable scientific and technological breakthroughs. The world was changed dramatically by new inventions that made life ever easier and more efficient.

▲ Geometric calculations
The ancient Egyptians were skilled mathematicians and made many new discoveries in geometry. For example, they knew how to calculate the height of a pyramid by measuring the length of its shadow on the ground.

◀ A Greek philosopher
Pythagoras of Samos (560–480BC) became one of the most highly respected Greek philosophers and teachers. Pythagoras believed that numbers were the perfect basis of life. He is most famous for his theory about right-angled triangles. This showed that if you square the two sides next to the right angle, the two add up to the square of the third side. (Squaring means multiplying a number by itself.)

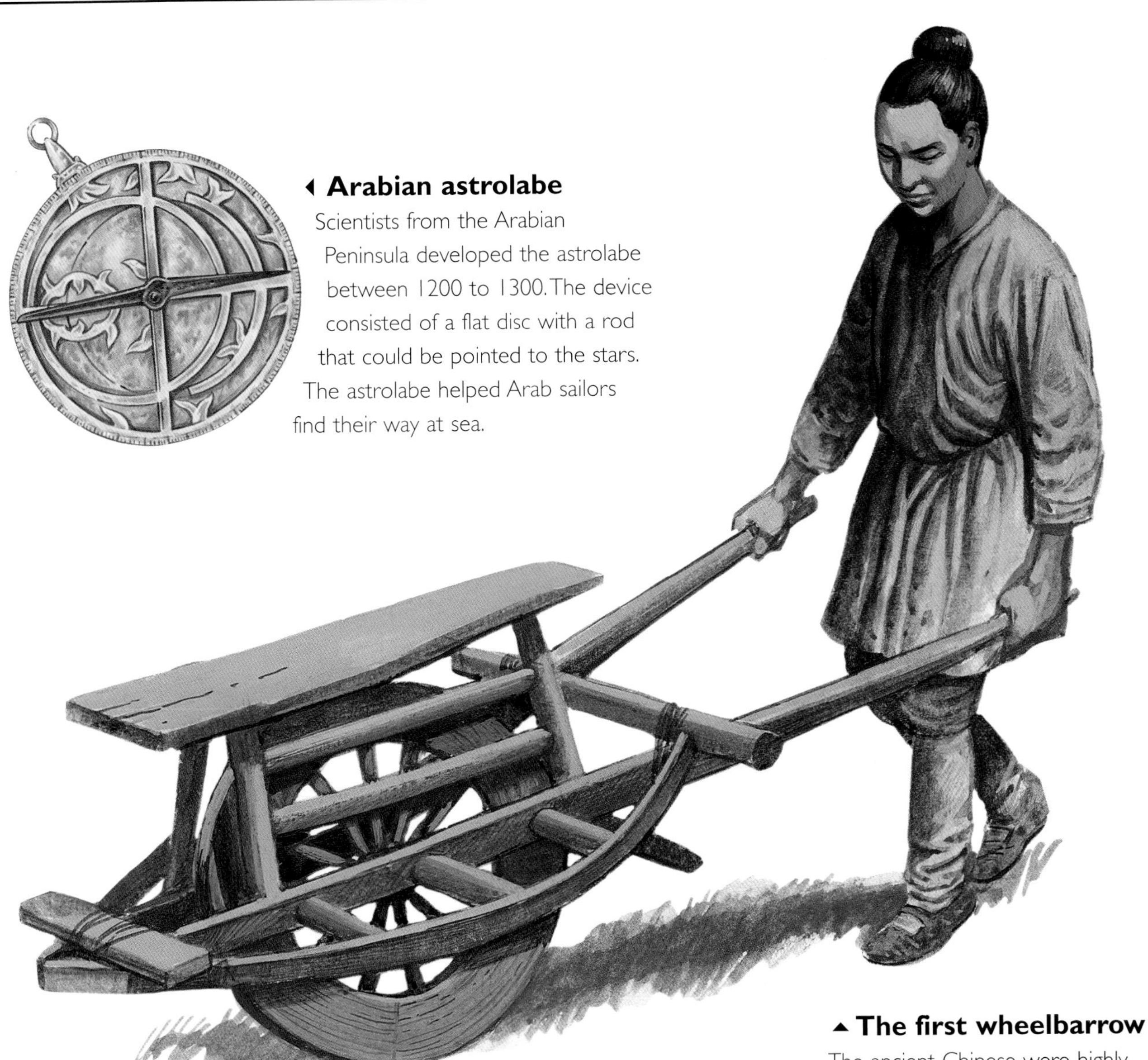

Arabian astrolabe

Scientists from the Arabian Peninsula developed the astrolabe between 1200 to 1300. The device consisted of a flat disc with a rod that could be pointed to the stars. The astrolabe helped Arab sailors find their way at sea.

The first wheelbarrow

The ancient Chinese were highly inventive. During the Han Dynasty (from 207BC to AD220), technological developments included the invention of the wheelbarrow, some 1,000 years before people in the West.

Remarkable roads

The Romans were some of the greatest builders and engineers of the ancient world. Their road-building methods were unsurpassed for centuries. They began building roads in 334BC. By the time the Roman Empire was at its peak, at around AD117, they had laid down more than 85,000km of roads.

Stone Age bow drill

Our ancestor, *Homo erectus,* learned to use fire at least 700,000 years ago. Early humans ate cooked food and had warmth and light at night. Fire was a useful way of keeping wild animals at bay and was also used to harden the tips of wooden spears. Hunters waving flaming branches could scare large animals into ambushes. Most archaeologists believe that *Homo erectus* did not know how to make fire but found smouldering logs after natural forest fires. Campfires were carefully kept alight, and hot ashes may have been carried to each new camp. Eventually, people learned that they could make fire by rubbing two dry sticks together. Then they found that striking a stone against pyrite (a type of rock) created a spark. By 4000BC, the bow drill had been invented. This made lighting a fire much easier.

YOU WILL NEED

Thick piece of dowelling (25cm long), craft knife, sandpaper, wood stain, paintbrush, water pot, balsa wood (8 x 8cm), modelling tool, self-hardening clay, rolling pin, cutting board, scissors, chamois leather, raffia or straw.

▼ The first match
One way early people made fire was to put dry grass on a stick called a hearth. Then they rubbed another stick against the hearth to make a spark and set the grass alight.

◀ Making dinner
Cave-dwelling *Homo erectus* people prepare to cook a meal in front of their cave. One member of the group makes stone tools, perhaps to cut up the dead animal. Another tends to the fire, and two children help an adult to dismember the carcass before it is cooked.

1 Shape one end of the piece of thick dowelling into a point with a craft knife. The blade of the knife should always angle away from your body when you cut the wood.

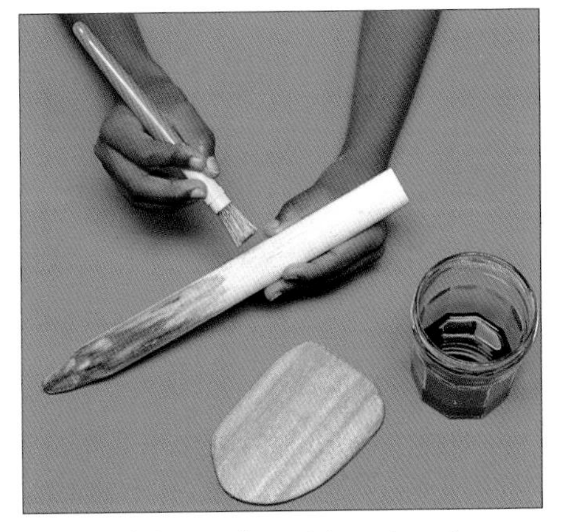

2 Sand down the stick and apply a coat of wood stain. Cut out the balsa wood base into a shape roughly like the one shown above. Paint the base with wood stain. Leave it to dry.

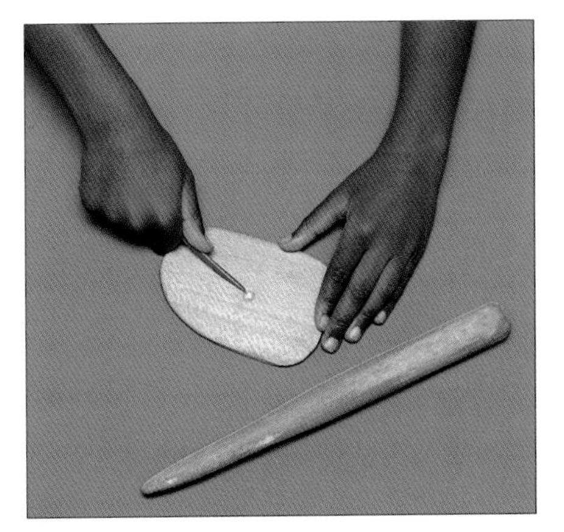

3 Use a modelling tool to gouge a small hole in the centre of the balsa-wood base. The sharpened end of the piece of dowelling should fit into this hole.

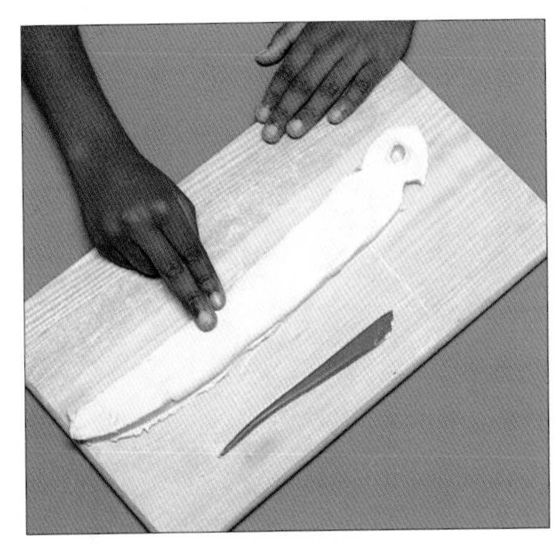

4 Roll out a piece of clay. Cut out a bone shape with a rounded end as shown above. Make a hole in each end of the bone and smooth the sides with your fingers. Let the bone shape dry.

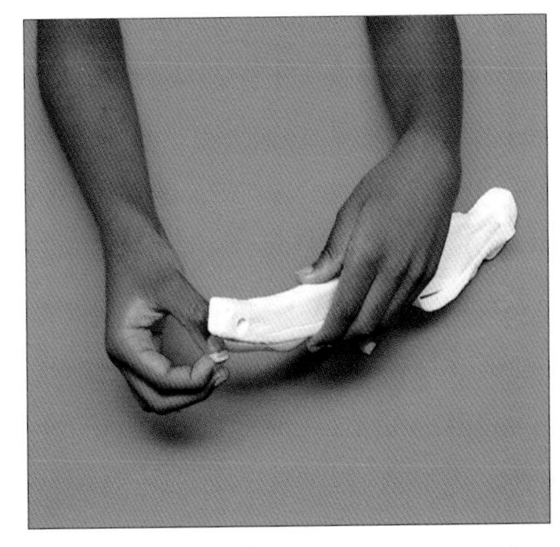

5 Use a pair of scissors to cut a thin strip of chamois leather twice as long as the bone. This will be the thong used to twist the bow drill. Tie the strip to one end of the bone.

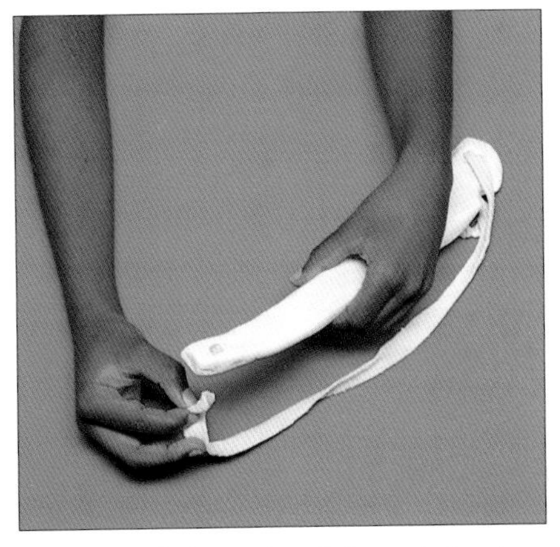

6 Thread the strip of chamois leather through the other hole. Tie a knot at the end to secure it. Now the bow piece is ready to be used with the drill you have already made.

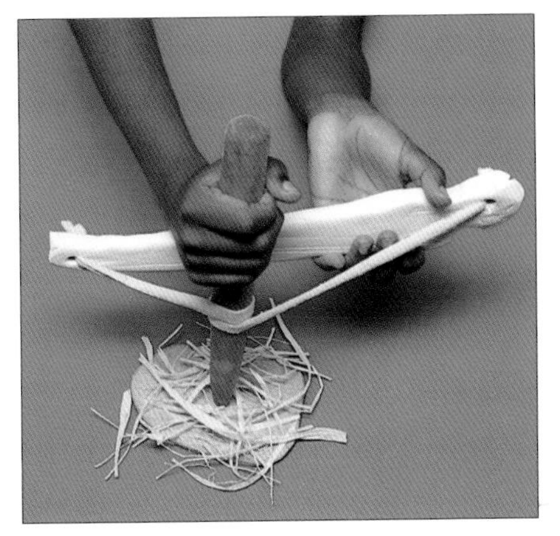

7 Scatter raffia or straw around the balsa wood base. Wrap the leather thong around the drill piece and place the pointed end of the drill in the hole on the base.

If you like, add a wood handle to the base to help you hold it. The bow drill you have made will not light real fires but shows you how Stone Age people spun a drill to make fire.

Egyptian shaduf

The ancient Egyptians called the banks of the River Nile the Black Land. This was because the river flooded each year in June, depositing a rich, fertile, black mud. The land remained under water until autumn. During dry periods of the year, farmers dug channels and canals to carry water to irrigate their land. A lifting system called a shaduf was introduced to raise water from the river. The success of this farming cycle was vital. Years of low floodwaters or drought could spell disaster. If the crops failed, people went hungry.

▲ Home on the Nile
Most ancient Egyptians lived close to the River Nile. The river was the main means of transport and provided water for their crops and their homes.

Templates

Cut out the pieces of card following the measurements shown.

A = irrigation channel and river bank
B = river
C = water tank

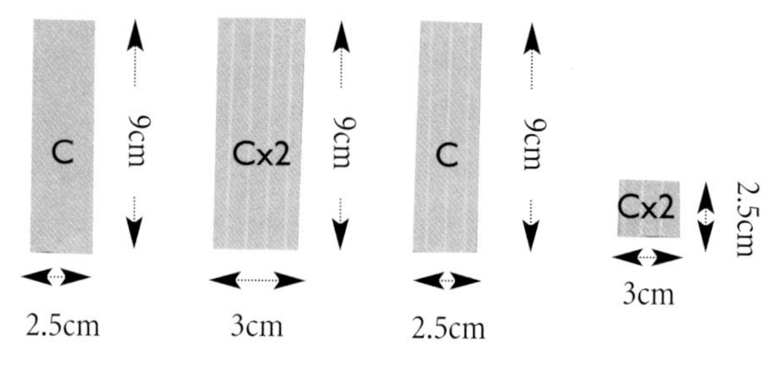

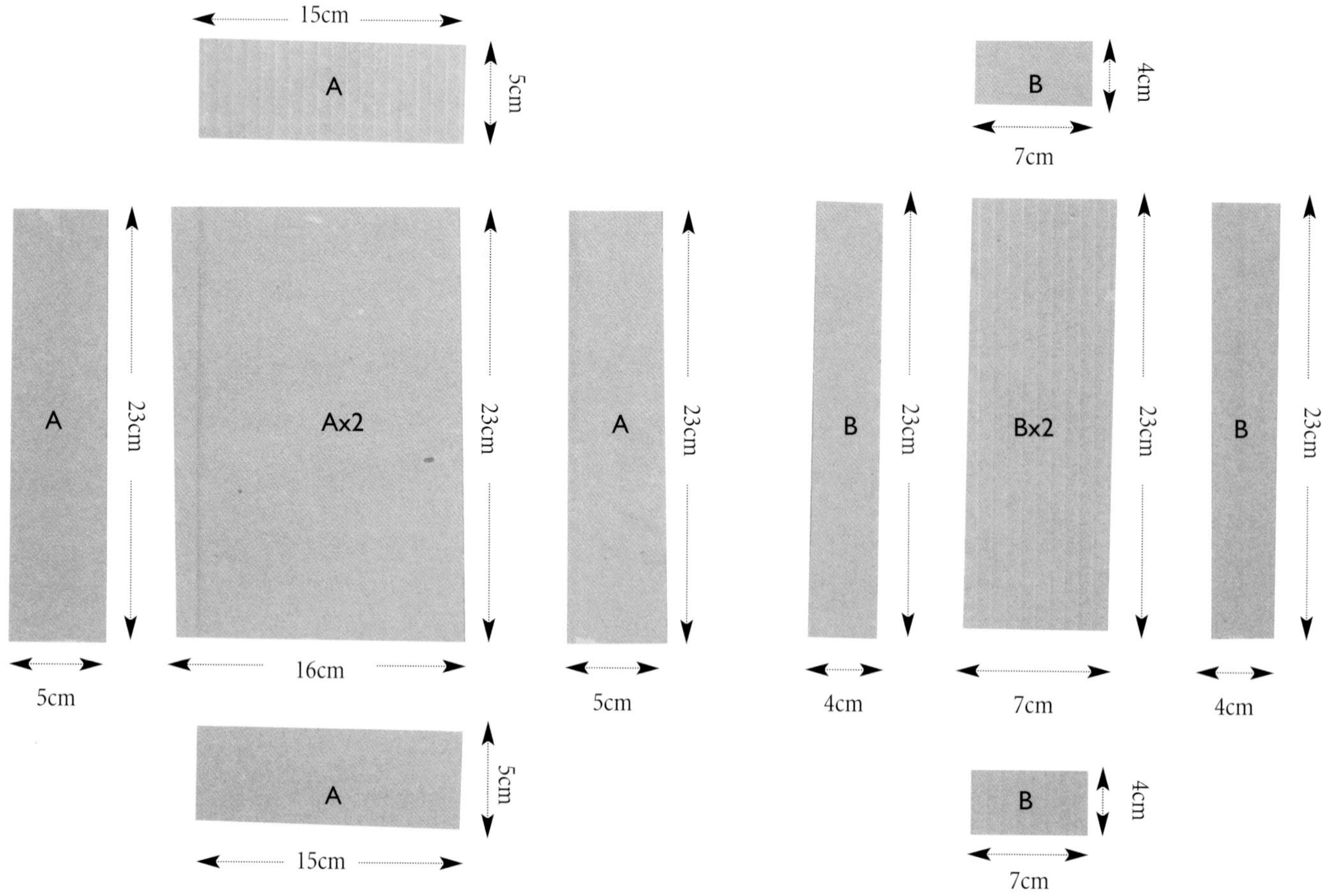

YOU WILL NEED

Card, pencil, ruler, scissors, PVA glue and glue brush, masking tape, acrylic paints (blue, green and brown), paintbrush, water pot, four balsa wood strips (two measuring 8cm and two 4cm), small stones, twig, self-hardening clay, hessian, string. Note: mix green paint with dried herbs for the grass mixture.

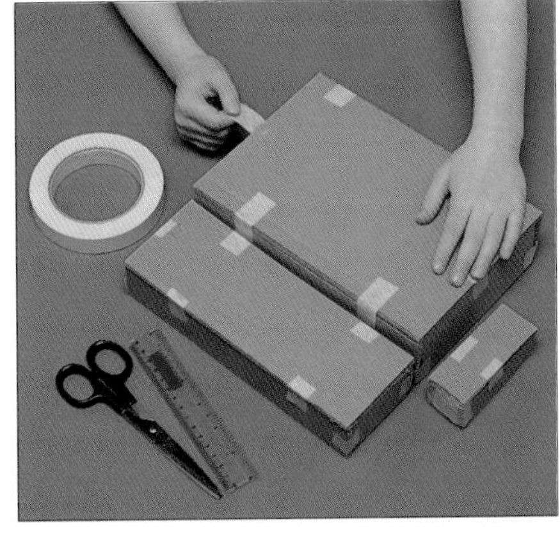

1 Glue the edges of boxes A, B and C as shown above. Secure them with masking tape until they are dry. Then paint the river section B and the water tank C blue and leave to dry.

2 Paint the box A with the green grass mixture on top, brown on the sides and the irrigation channel blue as shown. Next, get the balsa strips to make the frame of the shaduf.

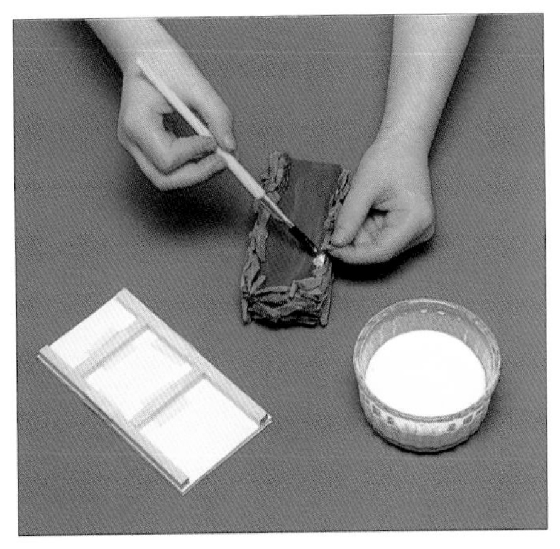

3 Glue the four balsa wood strips to make a frame. Support them with masking tape on a piece of card. When dry, paint the frame brown. Then glue the stones around the water tank.

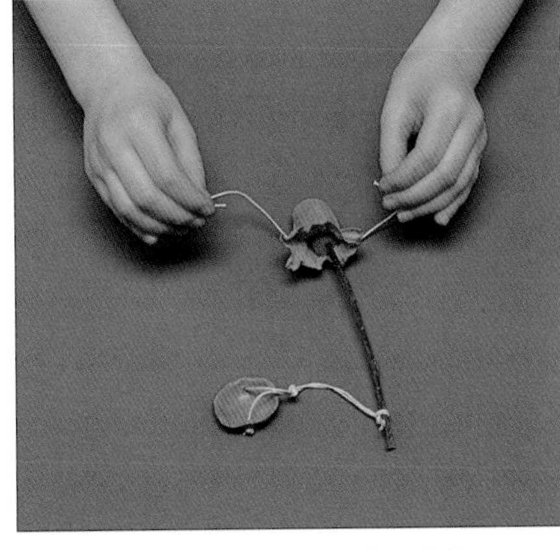

4 Use a twig for the pole of the shaduf. Make a weight from clay and wrap it in hessian. Tie it to one end of the pole. Make a bucket from clay, leaving two holes for the string.

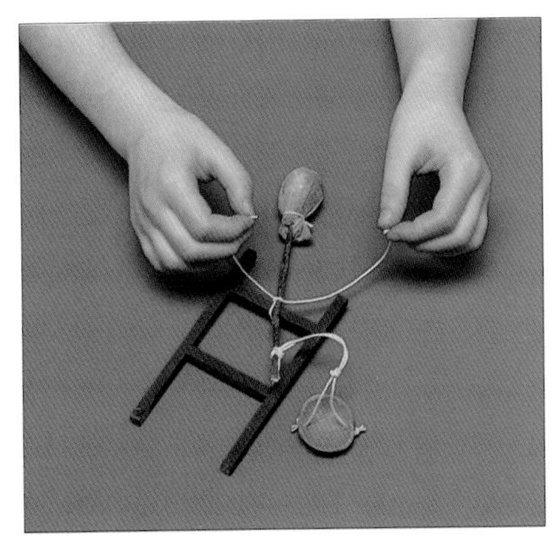

5 Using string, tie the bucket to the pole. Tie the pole, with its weight and bucket, to the frame of the shaduf. Glue the frame to the water tank, and then glue the tank to the riverbank section.

The shaduf was invented in the Middle East and brought into Egypt about 3,500 years ago. It has a bucket on one end of a pole and a heavy weight on the other. First, the weight is pushed up, lowering the bucket into the river. As the weight is lowered, it raises up the full bucket of water.

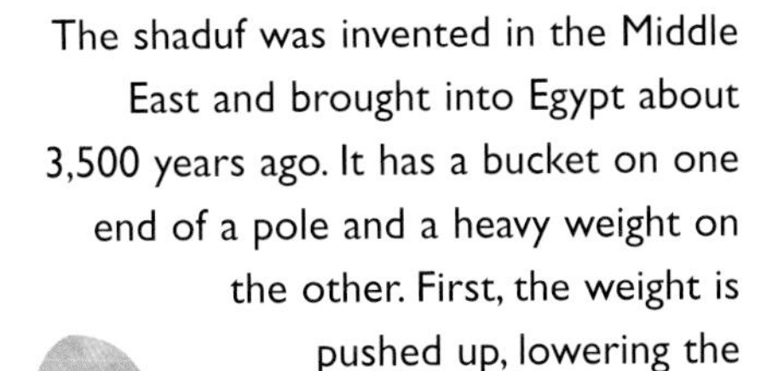

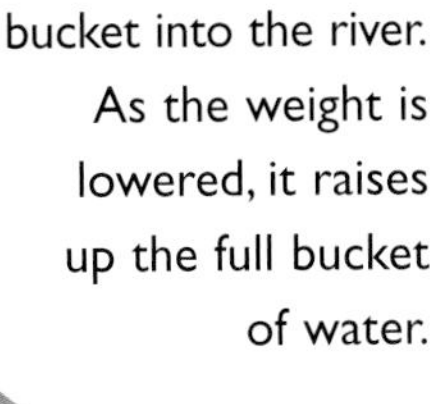

Archimedes' screw

The Greeks could afford to devote time to studying and thinking because their civilization was both wealthy and secure. They learned astrology from the Babylonians and mathematics from the Egyptians. They used their knowledge to develop many practical inventions, including water clocks, cogwheels, gearing systems, slot machines and steam engines. However, these devices were not widely used because there were many slaves to do the work instead.

Archimedes was the world's first great scientist. He came up with theories that could be proved or disproved by practical experiment or mathematical calculation. One of his most famous inventions, the screw pump, is still used in some places in the Middle East almost 2,000 years after this scientific breakthrough. The device is used to lift water from irrigation canals and rivers on to dry fields.

▲ Great inventor
Archimedes of Syracuse in Sicily was born around 285BC and spent most of his life in the city studying mathematics. He was killed when the Romans invaded Syracuse in 211BC.

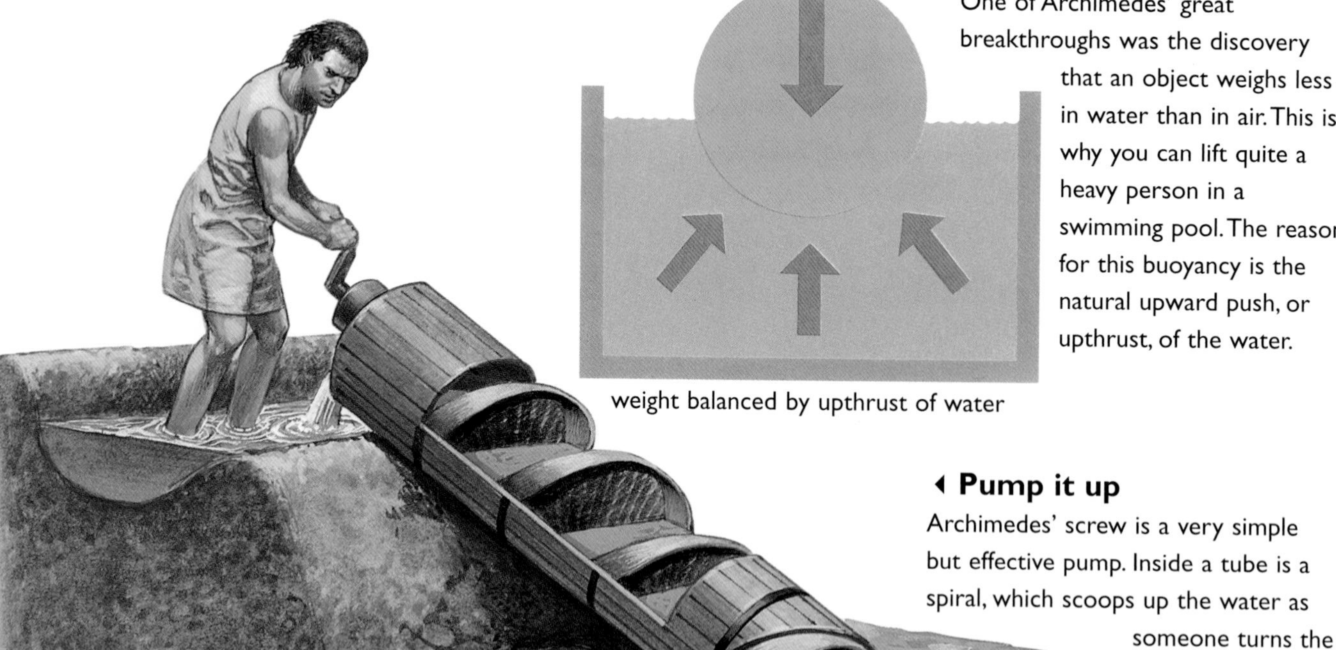

◀ Variable weight
One of Archimedes' great breakthroughs was the discovery that an object weighs less in water than in air. This is why you can lift quite a heavy person in a swimming pool. The reason for this buoyancy is the natural upward push, or upthrust, of the water.

◀ Pump it up
Archimedes' screw is a very simple but effective pump. Inside a tube is a spiral, which scoops up the water as someone turns the handle at the top.

YOU WILL NEED

Clean plastic bottle, scissors, self-hardening clay, strong tape, length of clear plastic tubing, bowl of water, blue food colouring, empty glass bowl.

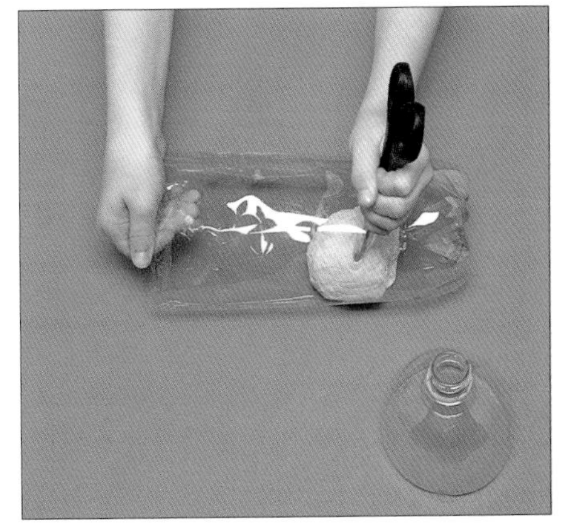

1 Cut off the top of the bottle. Put a lump of clay on the outside of the bottle, about 5cm from the end as shown. Punch a hole here with scissors and cut off the bottom of the bottle.

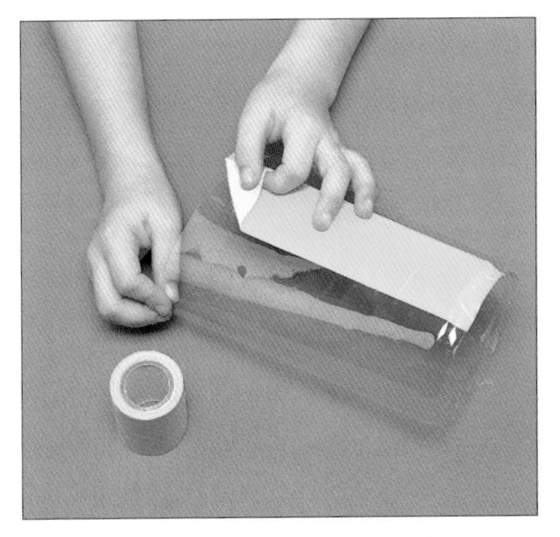

2 Cut a strip of strong tape about the same length as the bottle. Tape along the length of the cut bottle as shown above. The tape will give the plastic tubing extra grip later on.

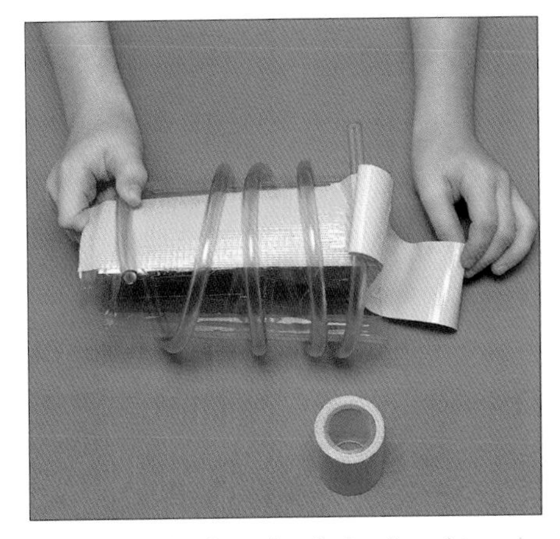

3 Twist the length of plastic tubing around the bottle from one end to the other as shown above. Secure the length of tubing in place with another piece of tape.

4 Place a few drops of blue food colouring into a bowl of water. Add the food colouring slowly and stir thoroughly so that the colour mixes evenly with the water.

The invention of the Archimedes' screw made it possible for farmers to water their fields from irrigation channels. It saved them having to walk back and forth between the river and fields with their buckets.

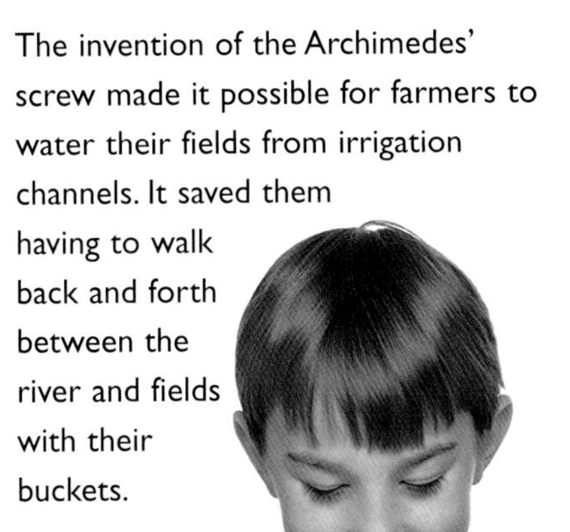

5 Place one end of the bottle and tubing construction into the bowl of coloured water. Make sure that the tube at the opposite end is pointing towards an empty bowl.

6 Twist the bottle around in the bowl of blue water. As you do so, you will see the water start to travel up the tube and gradually fill up the empty bowl.

Roman groma

The Romans were great builders and engineers. As the legions conquered foreign lands, they built new roads to carry their supplies and messengers. The roads were very straight, stretching across hundreds of kilometres. Romans used a groma to measure right angles and to make sure roads were straight. The roads were built with a slight hump in the middle so that rainwater drained off to the sides. Some were paved with stone. Others were covered with gravel or stone chips.

Roman engineers also used their skills to carry water supplies to their cities by building aqueducts. They built great domes, arched bridges and grand public buildings all across the Roman Empire, making use of whatever local materials were available. The Romans were also the first to develop concrete, which was cheaper and stronger than stone.

▲ ▼ **Travel in the Empire**
The Romans built strong stone bridges to carry roads high above rivers. Where ground was liable to flooding, they built embankments called aggers. Roman legions could move around the Roman Empire with astonishing speed thanks to the road system.

◀ **Building a road**
The Romans laid a deep solid foundation of large stones for their roads. They covered this with a smooth surface of flat stones, with a raised centre, or crown, so that rainwater could drain off at either side. They also dug ditches along the sides of the road to carry the water away.

YOU WILL NEED

Large piece of strong corrugated card, ruler, pencil, scissors, balsa wood pole, masking tape, card square, PVA glue and glue brush, non-hardening modelling material, aluminium foil, string, large sewing needle, broom handle, acrylic paints, paint brush, water pot.

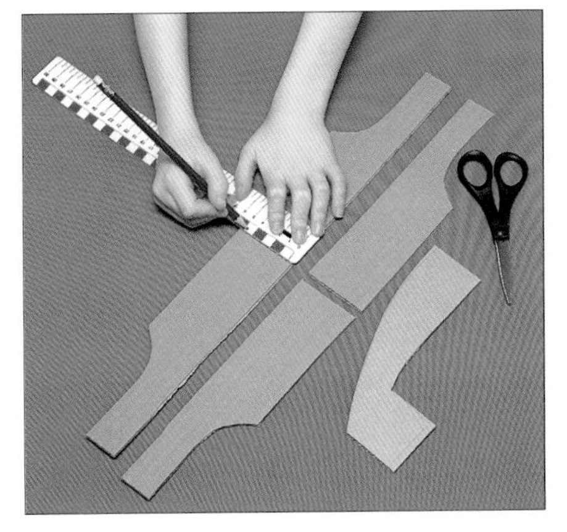

1 Cut three pieces of card, two measuring 20 x 6cm and one 40 x 6cm. Cut another piece at 15 x 12cm for the handle of the groma. Cut them into the shapes shown above.

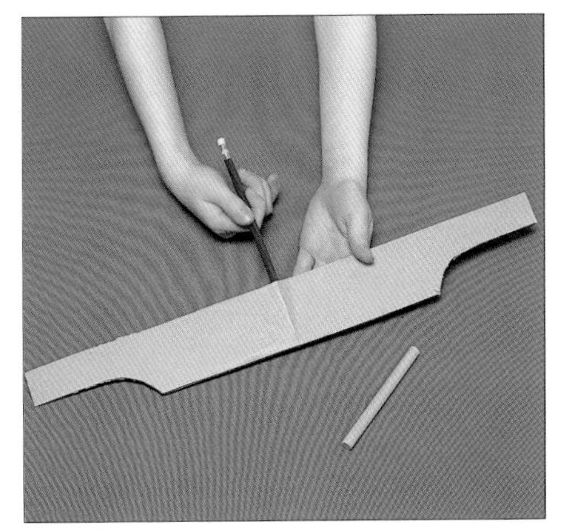

2 Measure to the centre of the long piece of card and use a pencil to make a slot here between the corrugated layers. The slot is for the balsa wood pole.

3 Slide the balsa wood pole into the slot and tape the card pieces in a cross. Use the card square to ensure the four arms of the groma are at right angles. Glue and secure with tape.

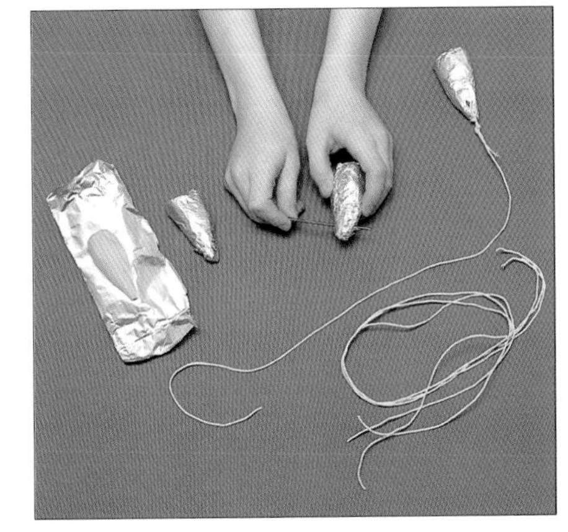

4 Roll lumps of modelling material into four small cones and cover each of them with aluminium foil. Then thread string through the tops of the cones to complete the plumblines.

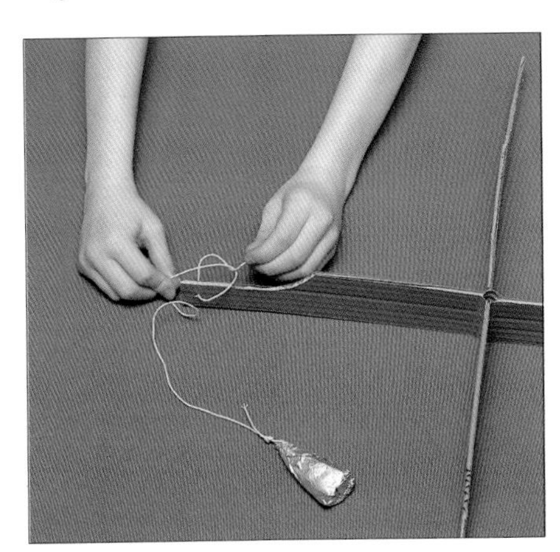

5 Make a hole at the end of each arm of the groma. Tie on the four plumblines. The cones must all hang at the same length – 20cm will do. If the clay is too heavy, use wet newspaper.

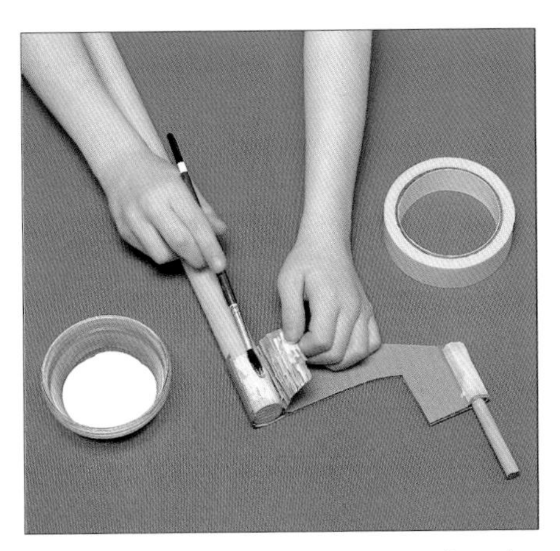

6 Split the top of the corrugated card handle piece. Wrap it around the balsa wood pole and glue it in place as shown. Split and glue the other end to the broom handle. Now paint the groma.

Slot the arms on to the balsa wood pole. Use the plumb lines as a guide to make sure the pole is vertical. The arms can be used to line up objects in the distance.

Viking coin and die

The Vikings were successful merchants. Their home trade was based in towns such as Hedeby in Denmark, Birka in Sweden and Kaupang in Norway. As they settled new lands, their trading routes began to spread far and wide. In about AD860, Swedish Vikings opened up new routes eastwards through the lands of the Slavs. Merchants crossed the Black Sea and the Caspian Sea and travelled to Constantinople (Istanbul), capital of the Byzantine Empire, and to the great Arab city of Baghdad. Viking warehouses were full with casks of wine from Germany and bales of woollen cloth from England. There were furs and walrus ivory from the Arctic and timber and iron from Scandinavia. Vikings also traded in wheat from the British Isles and rye from Russia.

▲ Trade exchange
The Vikings used coins for buying and selling goods at home, but they bartered items with their trading partners. In the East, the Vikings supplied furs, beeswax and slaves in exchange for silk, jewellery and spices.

▲ Trading nations
The routes taken by the Viking traders fanned out south and east from Scandinavia. Trade networks with the East linked up with older routes such as the Silk Road to China. Everyday items such as pottery and wool were brought back from western Europe.

YOU WILL NEED

Self-hardening clay, cutting board, rolling pin, pencil, thin card, pair of compasses, scissors, PVA glue and glue brush, bronze and silver paint, paintbrush, water pot, modelling tool.

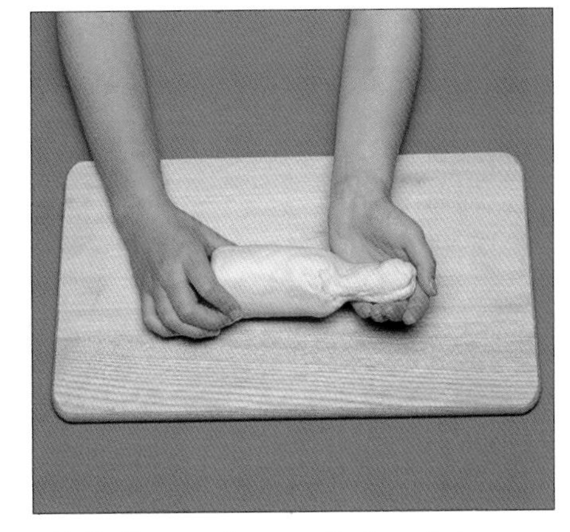

1 Roll out a large cylinder of clay on to a cutting board and model a short, thick handle at one end. This will be the die. Leave the die to dry and harden in a warm place.

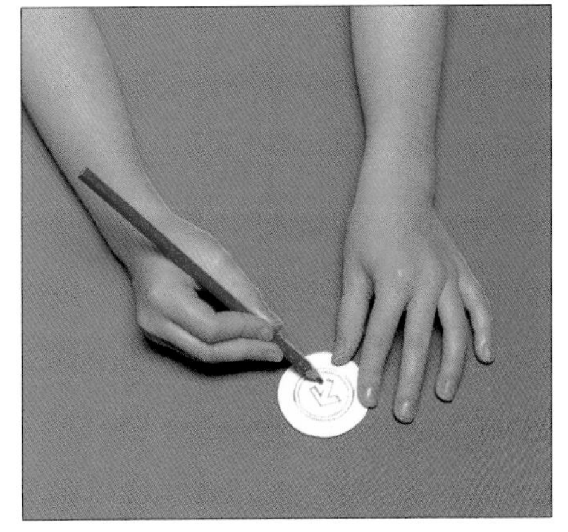

2 Draw a circle on a piece of thin card and cut it out. It should be about the same size as the flat end of the die. Use a pencil to draw a simple shape on the card circle.

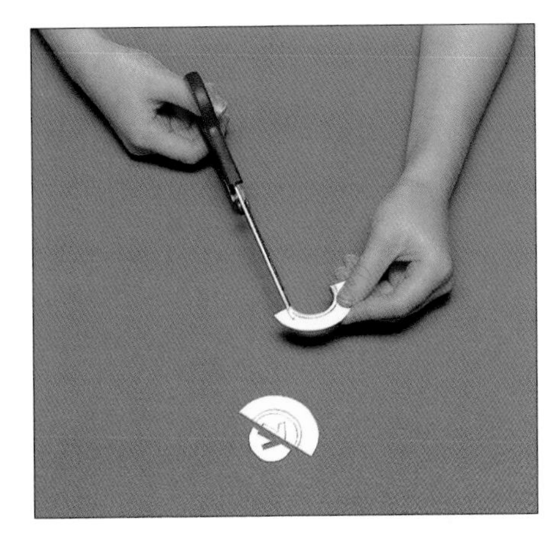

3 Cut the card circle in half and then cut out the shape as shown above. If you find it hard to cut out your coin design, you could ask an adult to help you.

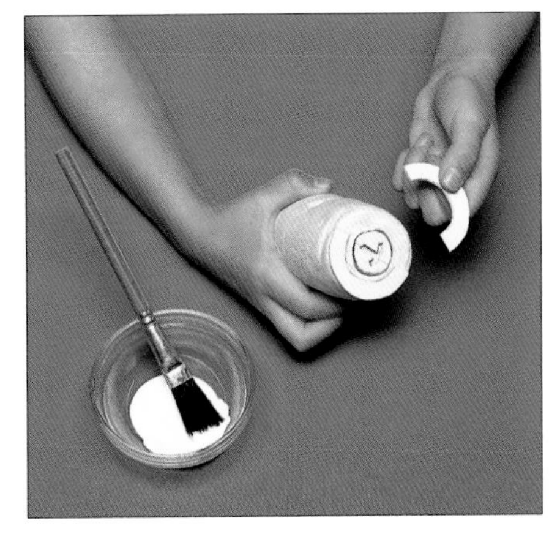

4 Glue the paper pieces on to the end of the die with PVA glue as shown above. You may need to trim the pieces if they are too big to fit on to the end.

5 Viking dies would have been made of bronze or some other metal. Paint your die a bronze colour to look like metal. Make sure you give the die an even coat of paint. Leave to dry.

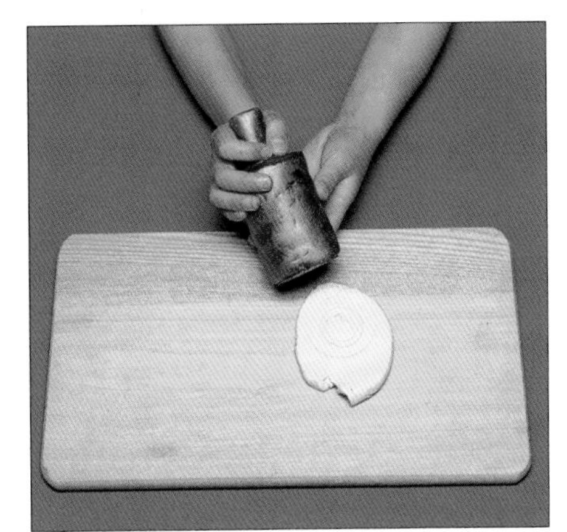

6 Roll out some more clay. Use the die to stamp an impression on to the clay. Use a modelling tool to cut around the edge of the circle, let the coin dry and then paint it silver.

A die is a metal stamp used to punch the design on to the face of a coin. The first coins showing Viking kings were made in England.

Mayan codex

The Maya were the first, and only, Native American people to invent a complete system of writing. They wrote their symbols in folding books called codices. These symbols were also carved on buildings, painted on pottery and inscribed on precious stones. Maya writing used glyphs (pictures standing for words) and also picture-signs that represented sounds. The sound-signs could be joined together – similar to the letters of our alphabet – to spell out words and to make complete sentences.

▾ Names of days

These symbols represent some of the names of the 20 days from the farmers' calendar. The 20 days made one month, and there were 13 months in a year. These symbols were combined with a number from one to 13 to give the date, such as 'Three Vulture'. Days were named after familiar creatures or everyday things, such as the lizard or water. Each day also had its own god. Children were often named after the day on which they were born.

YOU WILL NEED

Thin card, ruler, pencil, scissors, white acrylic paint, large paintbrush, water pot, eraser, tracing paper (optional), acrylic paints, palette, selection of paintbrushes.

1 Draw a rectangle measuring 100 x 25cm on to the piece of thin card and cut it out. Cover the rectangle with an even coat of white acrylic paint. Leave it to dry.

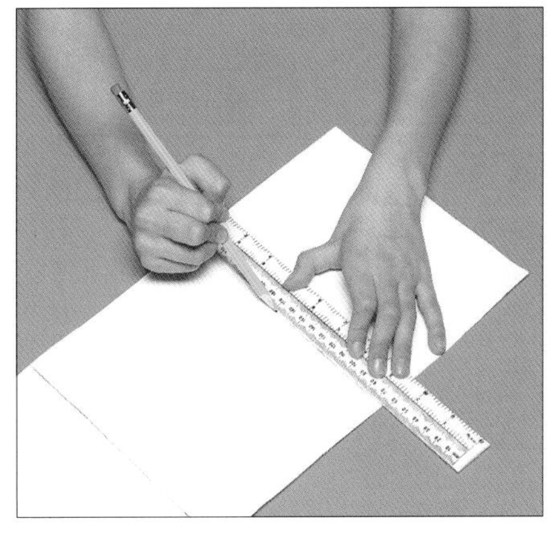

2 Using a pencil and ruler lightly draw in four fold lines, 20cm apart on the painted card, as shown above. This will divide the card into five equal sections.

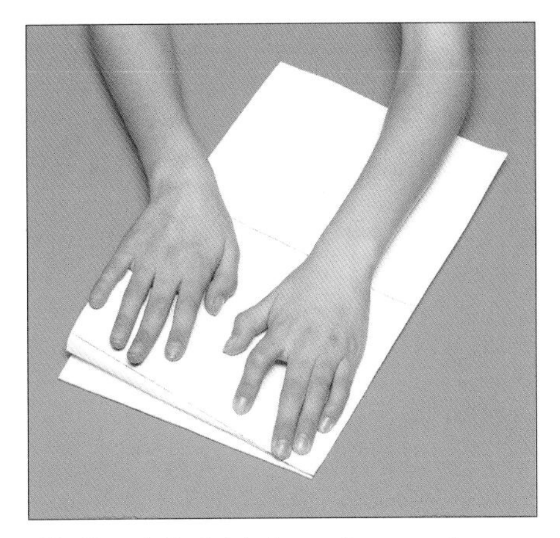

3 Carefully fold along the pencil lines to make a zig-zag book as shown in the picture above. Unfold the card and rub out the pencil lines with an eraser.

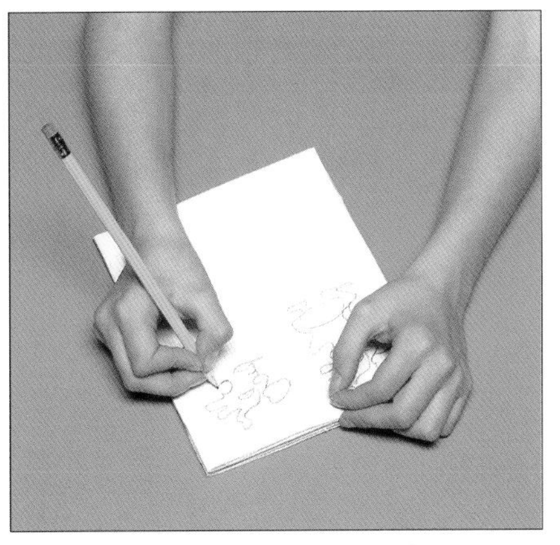

4 To decorate your codex you could trace or copy some of the Maya codex drawings from these pages. Alternatively, you could make up your own Mesoamerican symbols.

5 Paint your tracings or drawings using bright acrylic paints. Using the Maya numbers on this page as a guide, you could add some numbers to your codex, too.

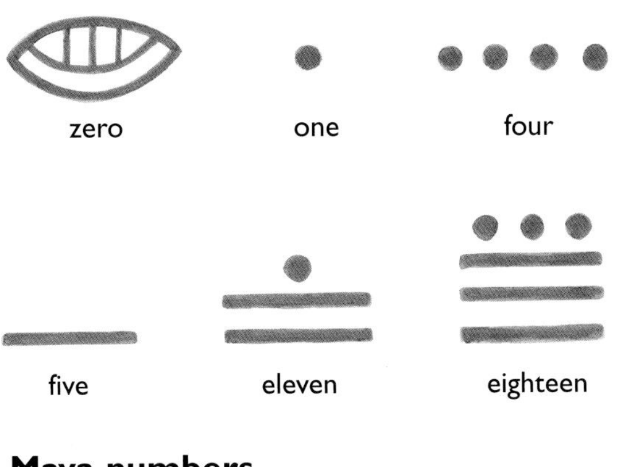

▲ Maya numbers
The Maya number system used only three signs – a dot for one, a bar for five and the shell symbol for zero. Other numbers were made using a combination of these symbols.

If you went to a Maya school you would find out how to recognize thousands of different picture-symbols. You would also be taught to link them together in your mind, like a series of clues, to find out what they meant.

Inca quipu

Inca mathematicians used a decimal system (counting in tens). One way of recording numbers and other information was on a quipu. Knots on strings may have represented units, tens, hundreds, thousands or even tens of thousands. To help with their arithmetic, people also placed pebbles or grains of maize in counting frames.

The Incas worked out calendars of twelve months by observing the Sun, Moon and stars as they moved across the sky. They knew that these movements marked regular changes in the seasons. Inca farmers used the calendar to tell them when to plant crops. Inca priests set up stone pillars outside the city of Cuzco to measure the movements of the Sun.

As in Europe at that time, astronomy, which is the study of the stars, was linked with astrology, which is the belief that the stars and planets influence human lives. Incas saw the night sky as being lit up by mythical characters. On dark nights, Inca priests looked for the band of stars that we call the Milky Way. They called it Mayu (Heavenly River) and thought its shape mirrored that of the Inca Empire.

▲ Star gazer
An Inca astrologer observes the position of the Sun. He is using a quipu. The Incas believed that careful watching of the stars and planets revealed their influence on our lives. They named one constellation (star pattern) the Llama. It was believed that it influenced llamas and those who herded them.

YOU WILL NEED
Waste paper, rope and string of various thicknesses, long ruler or tape measure, scissors, acrylic paints, paintbrush, water pot, 90cm length of thick rope.

1 Cut the rope and string into about 15 lengths, each measuring between 15cm and 80cm. Paint them in bright colours such as red, yellow and green. Leave them to dry.

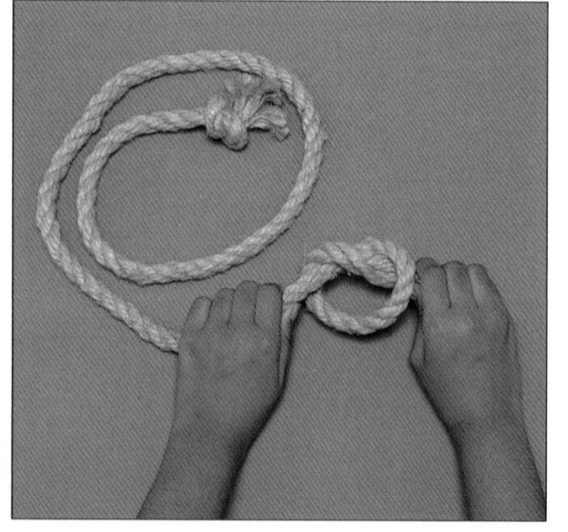

2 To make the top part of the quipu, take another piece of thick rope, measuring about 90cm in length. Tie a firm knot at each end of the rope as shown above.

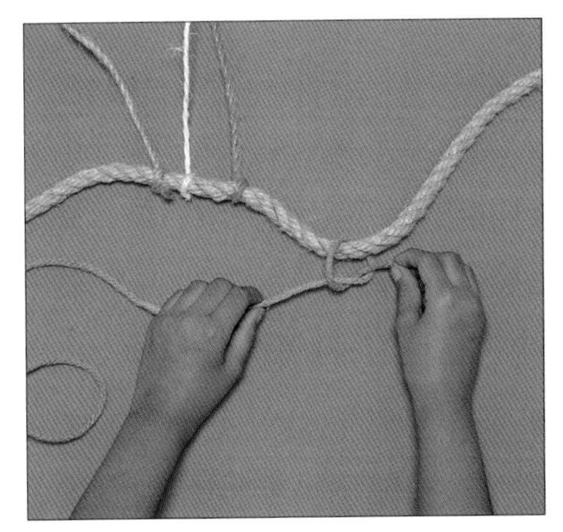

3 Next, take some thinner pieces of rope or string of various lengths and colours. Tie each one along the thicker piece of rope, so that they hang down on the same side.

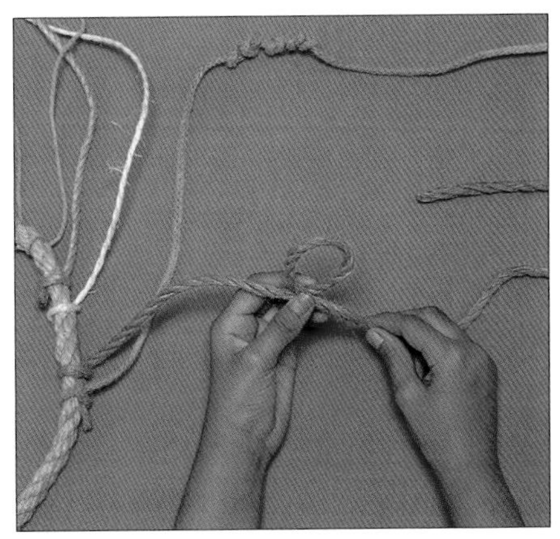

4 Tie knots in the thinner pieces of rope or string. One kind of knot that you might like to try begins by making a loop of rope as shown in the picture above.

5 Pass one end of the rope through the loop. Pull the rope taut but do not let go of the loop. Repeat this step until you have made a long knot. Pull the knot tight.

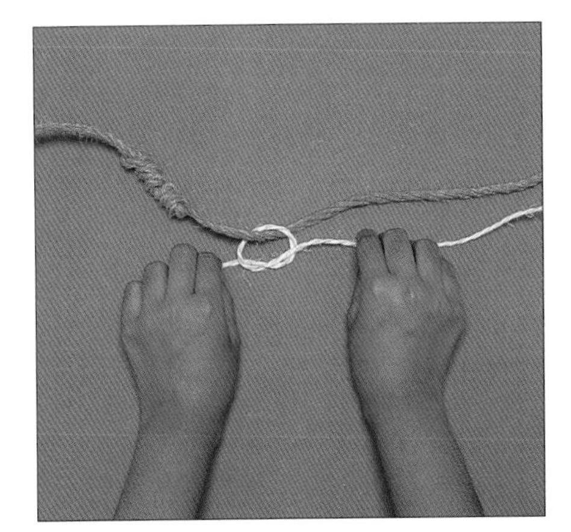

6 Make different sizes of knots on all the ropes and strings. Each knot could represent a family member, school lesson or other important details of your life.

7 Now add some more strings to the ones you have already knotted. Your quipu may be seen by a lot of people, but only you will know what the ropes, strings and knots mean.

Vast amounts of information could be stored on a quipu. The quipu was rather like an Inca version of the computer. Learning how to use the quipu and distinguish the code of colours, knots and major and minor strings took many years.

Illuminating letters

Before a way of printing words was invented in the late 1400s, the only way to have more than one copy of a book was to write it out by hand again. This was a time-consuming process and made books very valuable and rare. The pages were often beautifully illustrated with decorated letters like the one in this project. In Christian countries, many noble households had only one book, the Bible. Most books were kept in monastery libraries. In the 1500s, the only people who could read and write well were usually monks, priests or nuns. Kings and queens were also well educated.

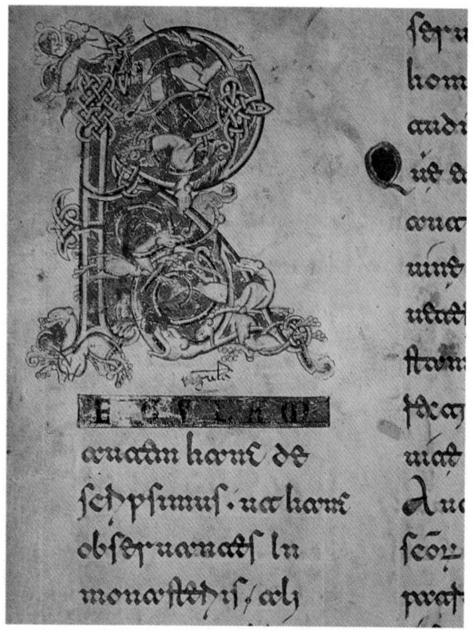

▲ **Lasting letters**
Many books were written on parchment, which was longer lasting than paper.

YOU WILL NEED

Pair of compasses, pencil, ruler, 16 x 16cm white art paper, eraser, acrylic paints, fine-tipped artist's paintbrushes, water pot, scissors, gold paint, PVA glue and glue brush, 26 x 26cm richly coloured mounting card.

1 Set your compasses to a radius of 6cm. Place the point at the centre of the 16 x 16cm white art paper and carefully draw a 12cm-diameter circle as shown above.

2 Keep the compasses at the same radius. Place the point 2cm away from the centre of the first circle. Then draw a second circle so that it overlaps with the first.

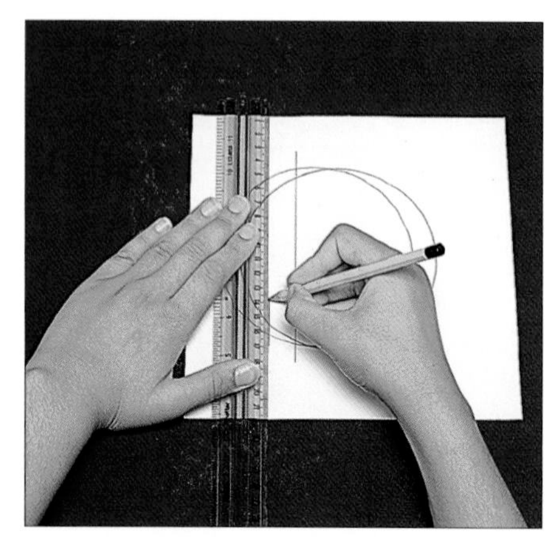

3 Place the ruler on the left-hand side of the overlapping circles. Draw two vertical lines from the top to the bottom of the circles. The lines should be around 2cm apart.

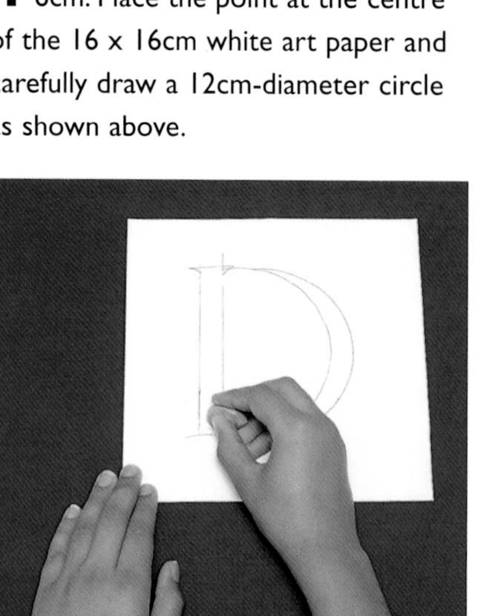

4 Rub out the lines of the circles to the left of the ruled lines. Use the ruler to draw two short lines to cap the top and the bottom of the vertical stem of the letter 'D'.

5 Extend the inner curve of the D into two squiggles at the top and bottom of the stem. Draw two simple spirals in the centre of the D as shown in the picture above.

6 Use the spirals to help you to fill in the rest of your letter design. Double the curving lines to make stems and leaves and add petals. Look at the picture above as a guide.

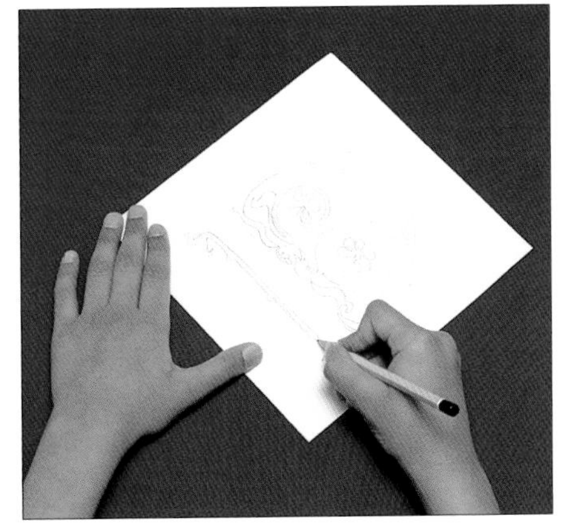

7 Draw two lines to the left of the vertical stem of the letter 'D'. Add a squiggle and leaves at the top and bottom and also some decorative kinks as shown above.

8 Use a pencil and ruler to draw a border around the letter about 1.5cm wide. Leave the right-hand side until last. See how the curve of the D tips out of the border.

9 First paint the border using a bright colour. Carefully fill in the whole design using other colours. Make sure that each colour is dry before you fill in the next one.

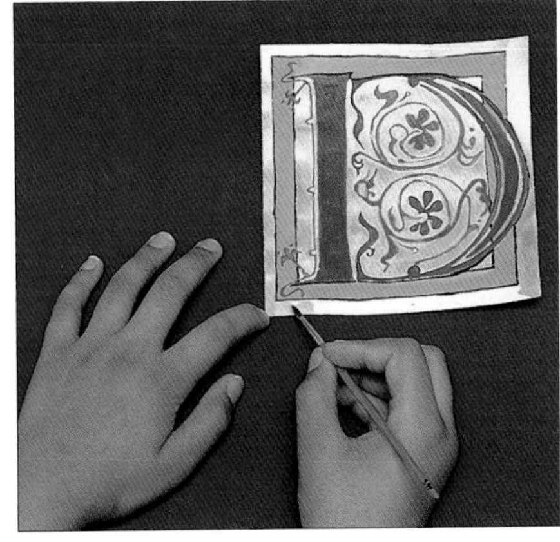

10 When the paint is dry, use a ruler and scissors to trim the whole artwork to a 15cm square. Then colour in the gold background. Leave it to dry on a flat surface.

11 Spread PVA glue over the back surface of the artwork. Then carefully place it squarely in the centre of the mounting card to add a richly coloured border to the letter.

In days gone by, there was lots to do before work could start. Animal skins were soaked, scraped and dried to make parchment. Feathers were sharpened into quills, and inks were mixed. Take time to draw and paint your illuminated letter. Monks and scribes were fast workers, but they still only managed to do two or three drawings a day. A mistake meant that the scribe would have to start again.

Pirate map

The area chosen for this map is the Spanish Main, which was a hotbed of pirates from the 1620s to the 1720s. When the Spanish first explored the Americas in the late 1400s, much of the surface of the Earth was unmapped territory. Consequently, many countries sent out naval expeditions to draw up detailed charts of distant waters for use by their trading ships. Most pirates had to make do with jotting down the details of the islands, coral reefs, coastlines and river mouths as they sailed by. Sometimes the pirates were lucky enough to capture a ship with up-to-date charts. Bound volumes of detailed nautical charts, known as waggoners, were a valuable prize for any pirate captain. When sailing into an unknown harbour, ships had to take a local guide or pilot on board – at the point of a sword if necessary.

YOU WILL NEED

Thick art paper, ruler, pencil, scissors, strong black tea left to cool, paintbrush, fine black felt-tipped pen, eraser, colouring pencils, large and small bottle tops.

1 Draw a rectangle on the paper, measuring 35 x 27cm. Cut it out, making the edges of the rectangle wavy and uneven to give the map an authentic aged and worn appearance.

2 Scrunch up the paper rectangle tightly into a ball. Then open and smooth it out on a flat surface. The creases will remain in the paper, giving the final map a used look.

3 Paint cold, strong tea on to the scrunched-up paper. The tea will stain the paper brown to look like old, worn parchment. Then leave the paper until it is completely dry.

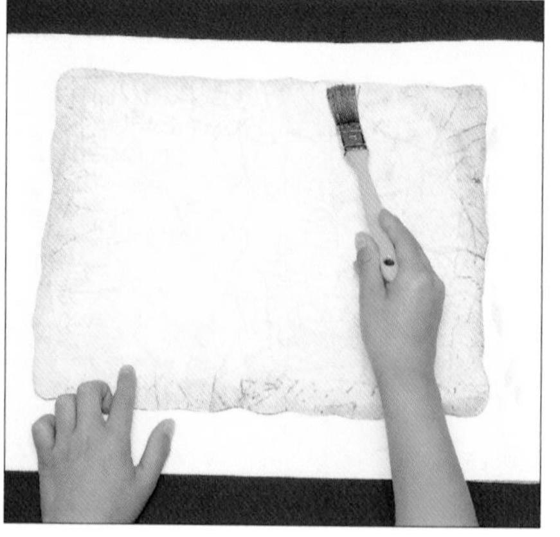

4 Smooth out the paper again. Stain the edges darker by brushing on more tea all the way around, from the outside inwards. Leave the paper to dry completely.

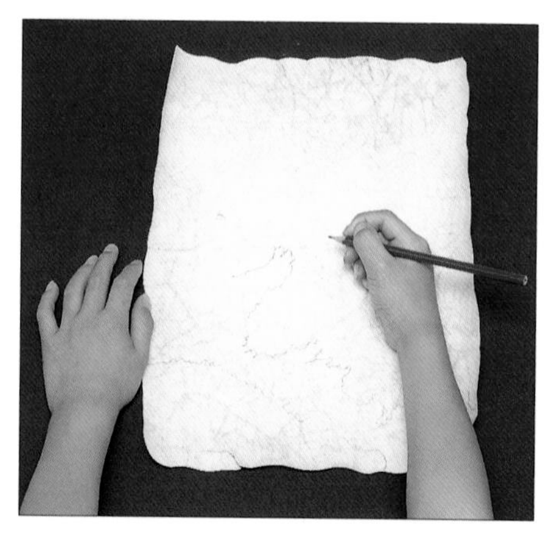

5 Copy the coastline from the finished map in step 12 using your pencil. If you prefer, you could make up your own map or trace a map from another book and use that instead.

6 Carefully draw over the coastline with your fine black felt-tipped pen. Make sure that you do not smudge the ink with your hand. Rub out the pencil lines with an eraser.

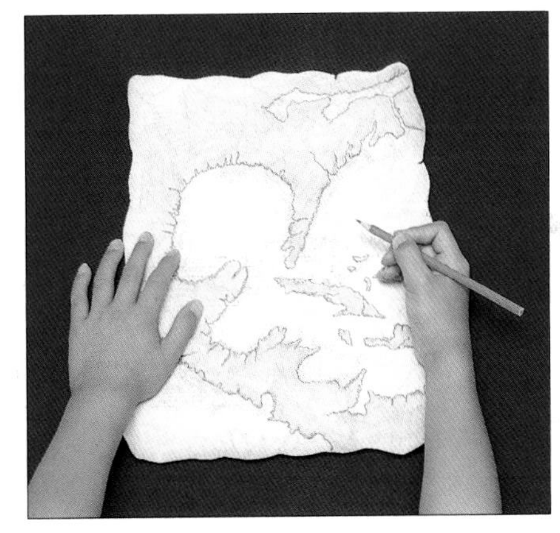

7 Colour the land green and the sea blue with your pencils. Graduate the colours, making them a little darker along the coastline and then fading inland or out to sea.

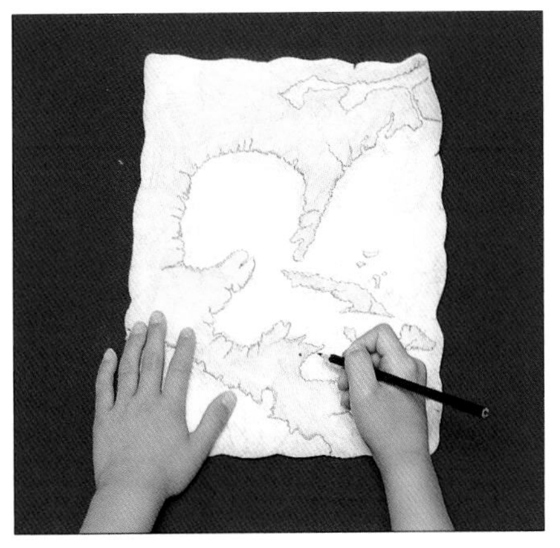

8 Choose three landmarks such as bays or headlands. Use the pencil and ruler to draw lines from the landmarks to a spot in the sea. This will mark your ship's position.

9 Use the ruler and a black pencil to draw straight lines across this position, or co-ordinate, as shown above. The resulting lines will look like the spokes of a wheel.

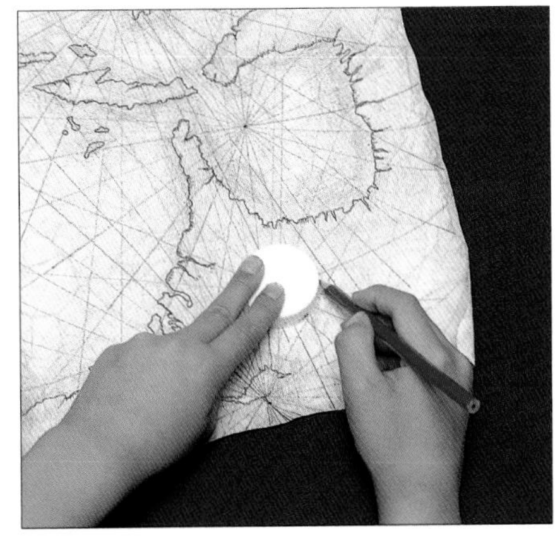

10 Draw around the large bottle top to make a circle on part of the map. Then draw an inner circle with the small bottle top to make a compass shape as shown.

The best maps for pirates would show safe ports and harbours, creeks and inlets. They also needed to show where there were dangerous coasts, currents and rocks. Maps had to be looked after so that they did not wear out with heavy use and in the damp conditions at sea.

11 Draw small, elongated triangles pointing outwards from the inner circle along the co-ordinate lines. Use bright colouring pencils to fill in the triangles on the compass.

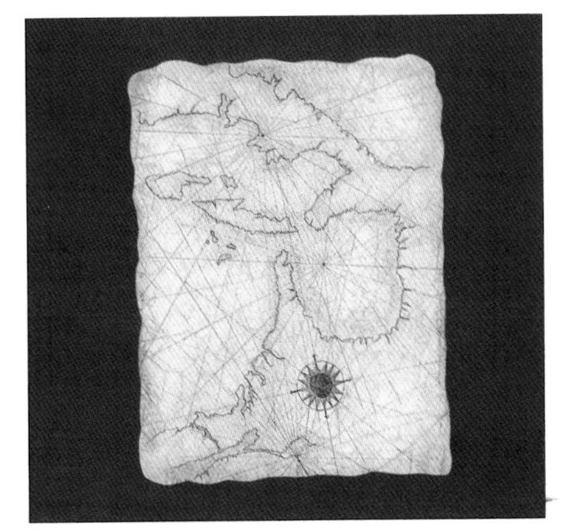

12 You can add more decorative details, such as arrow points on the compass, dolphins in the sea and treasure chests on the land. Your pirate map will then be complete.

Transport

People have often had to travel long distances for basic needs such as building materials, food and water. At first, everything had to be carried by foot, but the task was made much easier with the domestication of animals such as oxen and horses. These animals could be used to transport people and their goods. The invention of the wheel and of boats also revolutionized transport. Early vehicles, such as carts and sailing boats, enabled people to travel much greater distances across land and by sea. Heavy loads could be transported much more quickly, too.

▲ **Speed boat**
An Arctic hunter paddles his kayak. Sea kayaks were used to hunt sea mammals such as seals and walruses. These sleek, light one-person vessels were powered and steered by a double-bladed paddle. The design was so successful that kayaks are still used today.

▲ **Riding without stirrups**
Celtic leader Vercingetorix is seen here mounted on his horse. Big, strong horses were introduced into western Europe from the lands east of the Black Sea. These mounts gave Celtic hunters and warriors a great advantage over their enemies.

◀ **Camel caravan**
Arab merchants blazed new trails across the deserts. They traded in luxuries such as precious metals, gemstones and incense. The trading group, with its processions of camels, is known as a caravan.
Camels are well-suited to life in the desert. They have enlarged, flexible foot pads, which help to spread their weight across the soft desert sand.
Camels also have one or two humps on their backs, which contain fat and act as a food reserve.

◀ Hunting whales

This boat is known as an umiak. Teams of Inuit hunters used umiaks to hunt large whales. The oarsmen kept the boat steady so that skilled marksmen could launch harpoons at the whale. Umiaks were more stable than kayaks in rough seas, but they were much heavier to haul over the ice to the water's edge.

▼ Icemobile

A modern-day Inuit of the Arctic drives his scooter across the ice and snow. Scooters have largely replaced the traditional sledges pulled by dogs. For most present-day Arctic people, life is a mix of ancient and modern ways. Many Arctic groups use the new technologies of the developed world while holding on to the traditions and culture of their ancestors.

▲ High and mighty

A Mayan nobleman is carried in a portable bed known as a litter. This one is made from the hide of a wildcat called the jaguar. Spanish travellers reported that the Aztec emperor was carried in a litter, too. Blankets were also spread in front of the emperor as he walked, to stop his feet touching the ground.

Sumerian coracle

The ancient region of Mesopotamia was situated on the Tigris and Euphrates rivers and their tributaries. The rivers formed a vital transport and communications network around the country. The Sumerians lived in the south of Mesopotamia around 6,000 years ago. Later on, the land in north Mesopotamia became known as Assyria. The boat in this project is modelled on a Sumerian coracle. These boats were made from leather stretched over a wooden frame.

YOU WILL NEED

Self-hardening clay, wooden board, ruler, cocktail stick, paper, acrylic paints, paintbrush, water pot, piece of dowelling measuring about 20cm long, PVA glue and glue brush, water-based varnish and brush, string, scissors.

◂ Rowing the boat
The Phoenicians lived by the Mediterranean Sea to the west of Mesopotamia. They were the great sailors and shipbuilders of the time. Their ships were large and many-oared, and the sailors worked out how to navigate using the stars.

▴ Built on the banks
The ancient city of Nimrud, on the banks of the River Tigris, was part of the Assyrian Empire. Archaeologists have found the remains of several palaces and temples here.

1 Make a dish shape using the self-hardening clay. It should be about 14cm long, 11cm wide and 4cm deep. Make a mast hole for the dowelling mast. Attach it to the base.

2 Trim the excess clay around the top of the boat to smooth it out. Use a cocktail stick to make four small holes through the sides of the boat. Let the clay dry out completely.

3 When it is dry, paint the boat a light brown base colour. Cover the work surface with paper. Then use a brush and your fingers to flick contrast colours and create a mottled effect.

4 Put a drop of glue inside the mast hole. Put more glue around the end of the dowelling mast and then push it into the hole. The mast should stand upright in the centre of the clay boat.

5 Wait until the glue has dried and the mast stands firm. Then paint a layer of water-based varnish all over your boat. Let the first layer dry and then paint another layer over it.

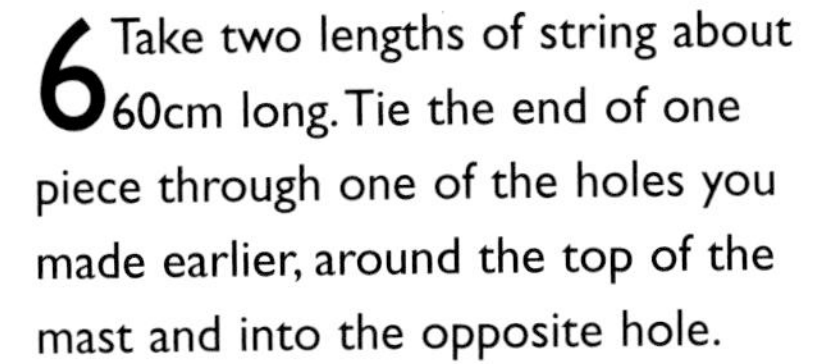

6 Take two lengths of string about 60cm long. Tie the end of one piece through one of the holes you made earlier, around the top of the mast and into the opposite hole.

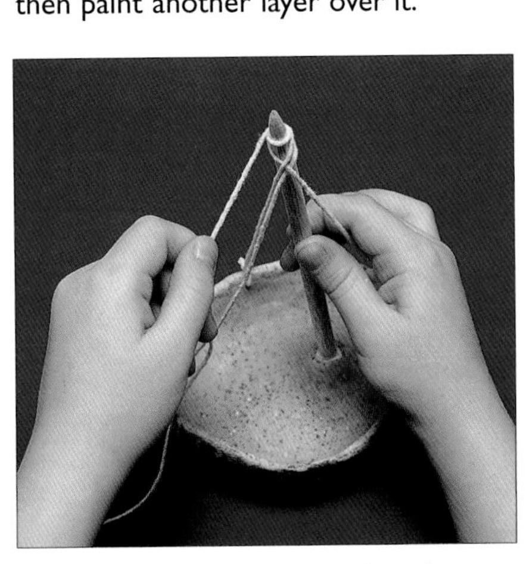

7 Complete the rigging of the boat by tying the other piece of string through the empty holes and around the top of the mast as before. Trim off the excess string.

Coracles, such as the one you have made, had a mast for a light sail. It was probably steered using oars or a punt pole. Small boats such as these are still used today on the River Euphrates.

Assyrian chariot

The wooden wheel was first used as a means of transport around 5,500 years ago in what is now the Middle East, and the news spread fast in neighbouring regions. In Sumerian times (3000–2000BC), wild asses hauled chariots, while oxen and mules were used for heavy loads. By about 900BC, the time of the Assyrian Empire, spoked wheels had replaced the earlier wheels made from a single piece of solid wood.

Roads varied in quality through the Assyrian Empire. Local paths were little more than tracks, but there were good roads between the main towns. These were well-maintained so that messengers and state officials could reach their destination quickly. The Assyrians also perfected the art of chariot warfare, which gave them a big advantage over enemies who were fighting on foot. They could attack their enemies from above, and were able to move around the battlefield quickly.

▲ Unstoppable warriors
Chariots were mainly used by Assyrian kings and their courtiers when hunting and in battle. At rivers, the chariots were dismantled and carried across on boats, and people swam across using inflated animal skins as life belts.

▲ Wheeled procession
An artist's impression of a Sumerian funeral procession shows the solid wood wheel design of the early chariots in Mesopotamia. Rituals involving death and burial were an important part of Sumerian life.

▲ Education of a prince
Learning to drive a chariot and fight in battle were part of King Ashurbanipal's education as crown prince of Assyria. He was also taught foreign languages, how to ride a horse and hunt.

YOU WILL NEED

Thick card, pair of compasses, ruler, pencil, scissors, pen, masking tape, newspaper, two card tubes, flour and water (for papier mâché), cream and brown acrylic paints, paintbrush, water pot, two pieces of dowelling measuring 16cm long, needle, four cocktail sticks.

1 Measure and cut out four card circles, each one measuring 7cm in diameter. Carefully use the scissors to make a hole in the centre of each circle. Enlarge the holes with a pen.

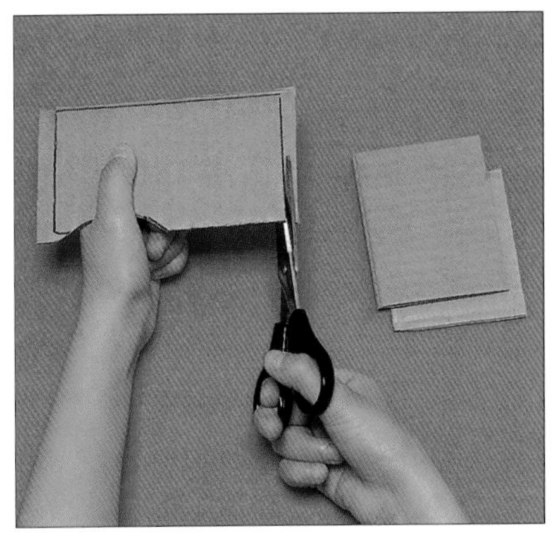

2 Cut out two sides for the chariot, 12cm long and 7.5cm wide as shown, one back 9 x 7.5cm, one front 15 x 9cm, one top 9 x 7cm and one base 12 x 9cm.

3 Trim the top of the front to two curves as shown above. Stick the side pieces to the front and back using masking tape. Then stick on the base and the top of the chariot.

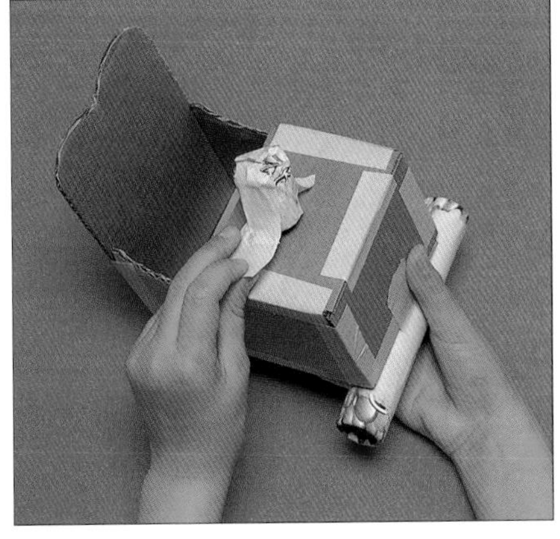

4 Roll up a piece of old newspaper to make a cylinder shape about 2.5cm long and tape it to the chariot as shown above. Attach the card tubes to the bottom of the chariot.

5 Mix a paste of flour and water. Dip newspaper strips into the paste to make papier mâché. Cover the chariot with layers of papier mâché until the card underneath is hidden. Let it all dry.

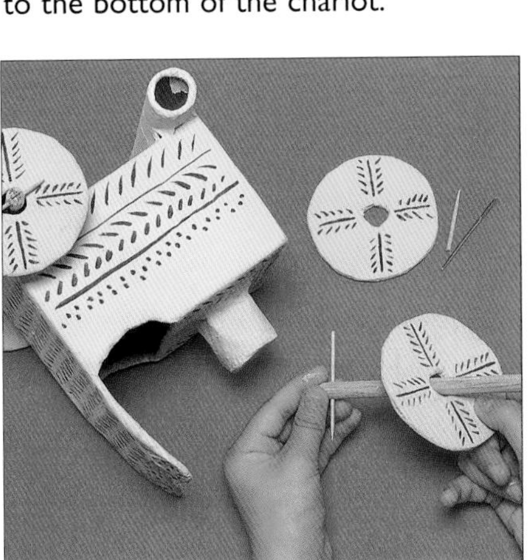

6 Paint the chariot. Use a needle to make a hole at each end of a piece of dowelling. Insert a cocktail stick, add a wheel and insert into the tube. Secure another wheel at the other end. Repeat.

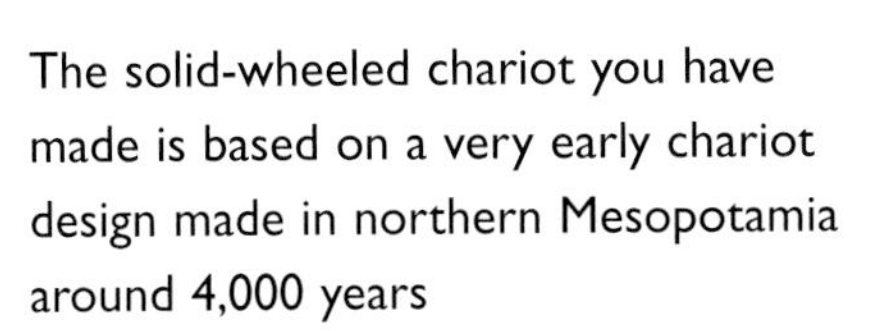

The solid-wheeled chariot you have made is based on a very early chariot design made in northern Mesopotamia around 4,000 years ago. When the spoked wheel replaced the solid wheel, chariots became lighter, faster and easier to steer.

Chinese sampan

From early in China's history, its rivers, lakes and canals were its main highways. Fisherfolk propelled small wooden boats across the water with a single oar or pole at the stern. These were often roofed with mats, like the sampans still seen today. Large wooden sailing ships, which we call junks, sailed the open ocean. They were either keeled or flat-bottomed, with a high stern and square bows. Their sails were made of matting stiffened with strips of bamboo.

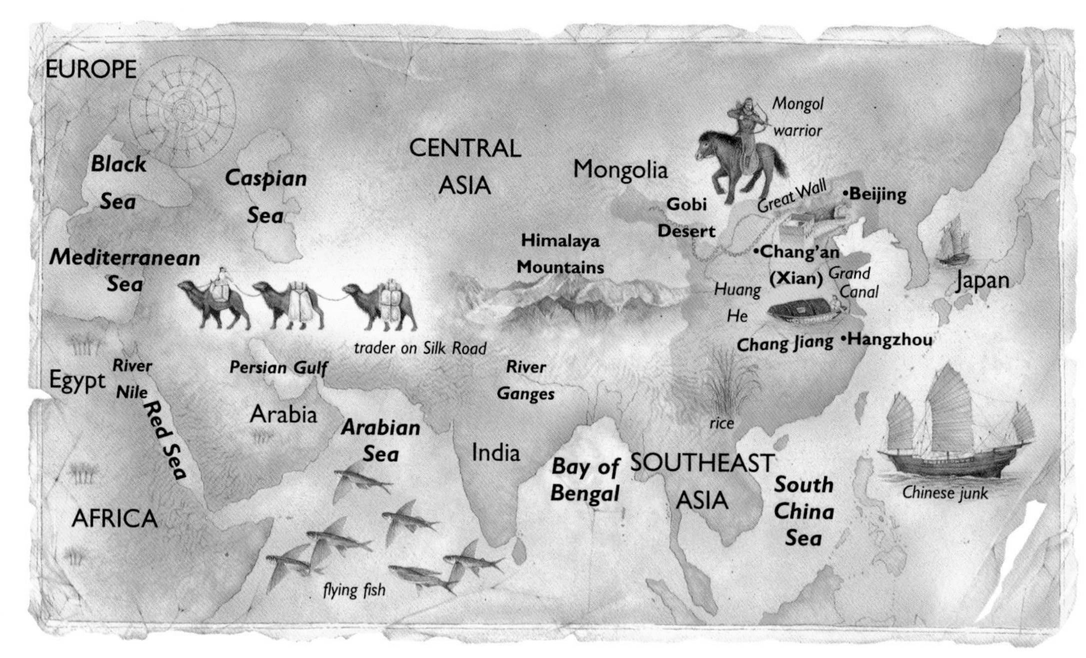

▲ Trading places
The map shows the extent of the Chinese Empire during the Ming Dynasty (1368–1644). Merchants transported luxury Chinese goods along the Silk Road, from Chang'an (Xian) to the Mediterranean Sea. Chinese traders also sailed across the South China Sea to Vietnam, Korea and Japan.

Templates

Cut templates B, C, D and G from thick card. Cut templates A, E and F from thin card.

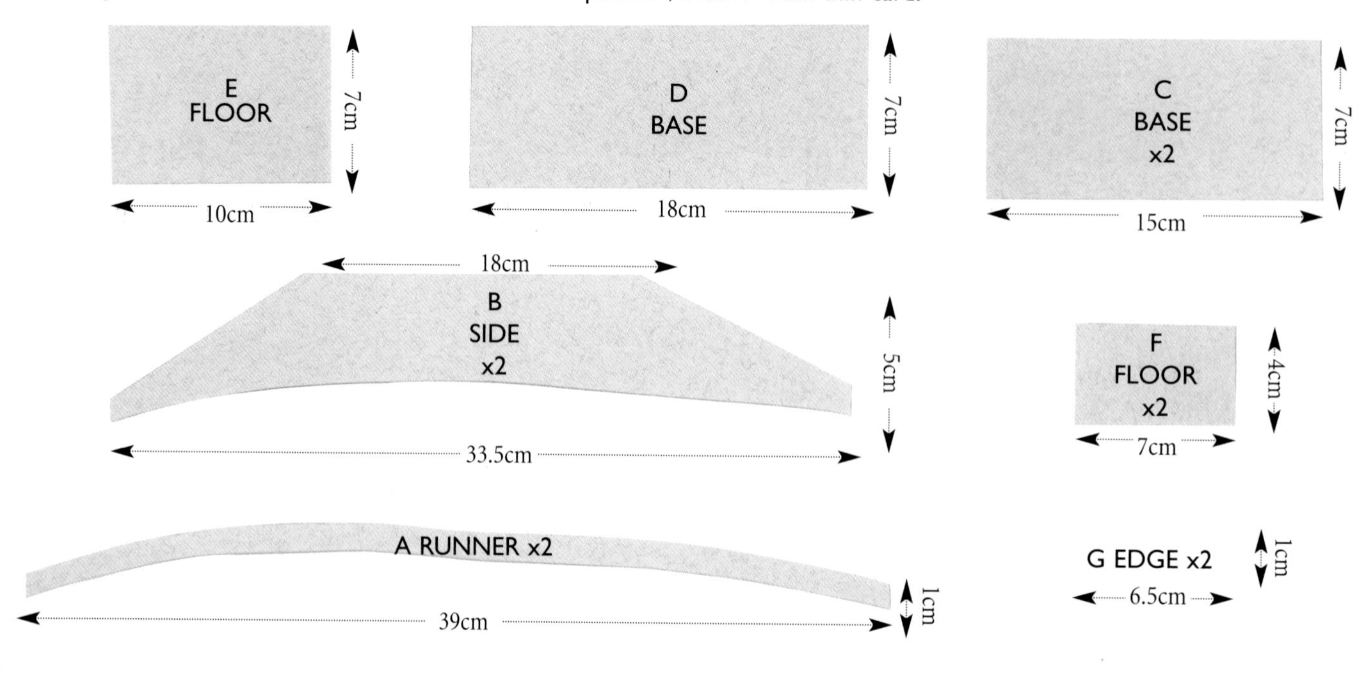

YOU WILL NEED

Thick card, thin card, ruler, pencil, scissors, PVA glue and glue brush, masking tape, seven wooden barbecue sticks, string, thin yellow paper, acrylic paints (black and dark brown), paintbrush and water pot.

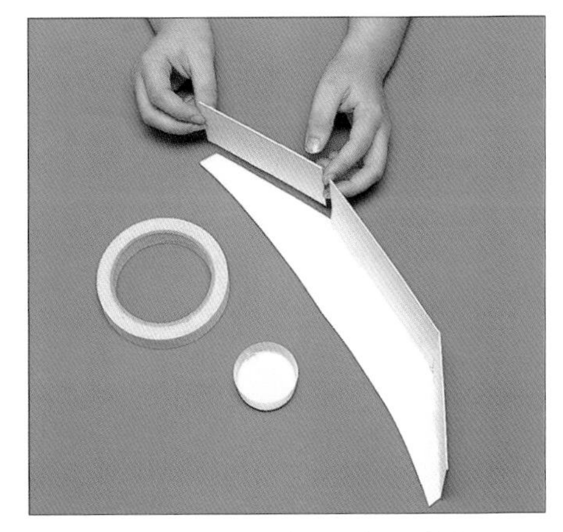

1 Glue base templates C and D to side template B as shown. Hold the pieces together with strips of masking tape while the glue dries. When dry, remove the masking tape.

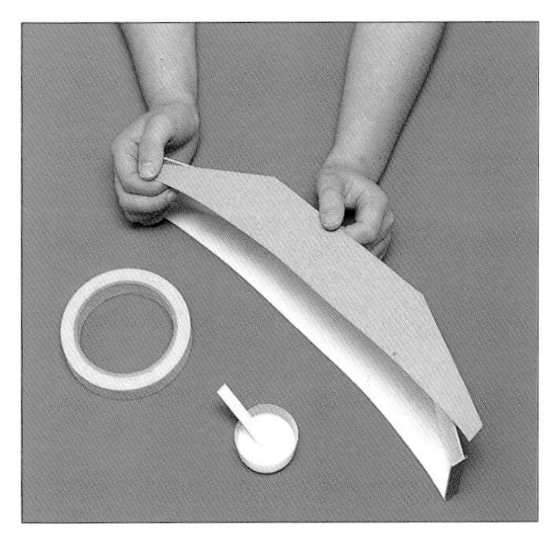

2 Glue the remaining side B to the boat. Stick the runner A pieces to the top of the sides and secure with masking tape. Make sure the ends jut out at the front and back of the boat.

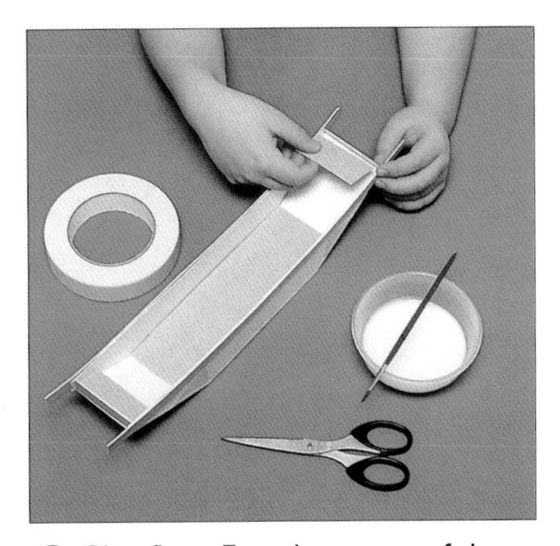

3 Glue floor E to the centre of the base. Add the floor F templates to the ends of the base. Stick the edge G templates in between the edge of the runners and leave to dry.

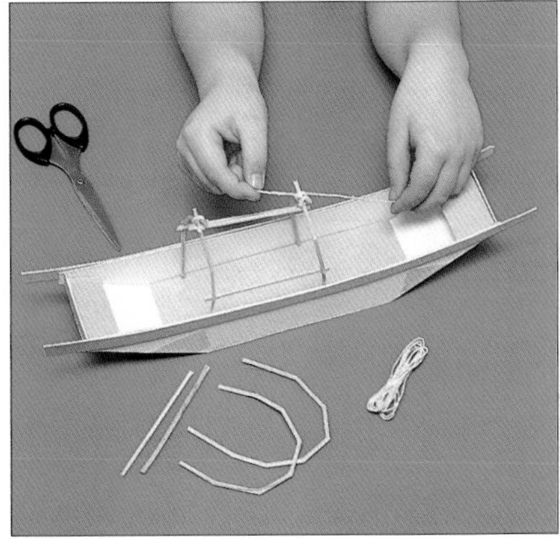

4 Bend two barbecue sticks into arches. Cut two sticks into struts. Tie struts to the sides and top of the arches. Make a second roof by bending three barbecue sticks into arches.

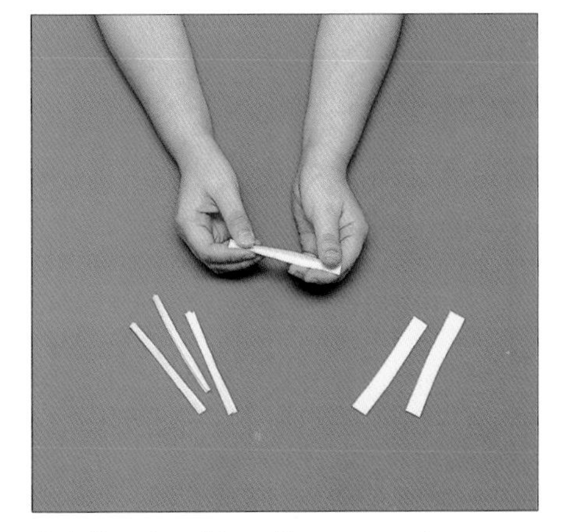

5 Cut the thin yellow paper into strips, each measuring 10 x 1cm. Fold the strips in half as shown. The strips will make the matting for the two boat roofs.

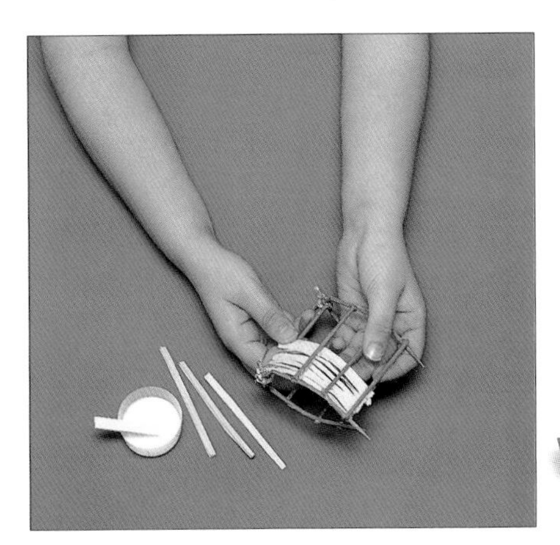

6 Paint the boat and the roof sections and allow them to dry. Glue the roof matting strips to the inside of the roofs. When the glue is dry, place the roofs inside the boat.

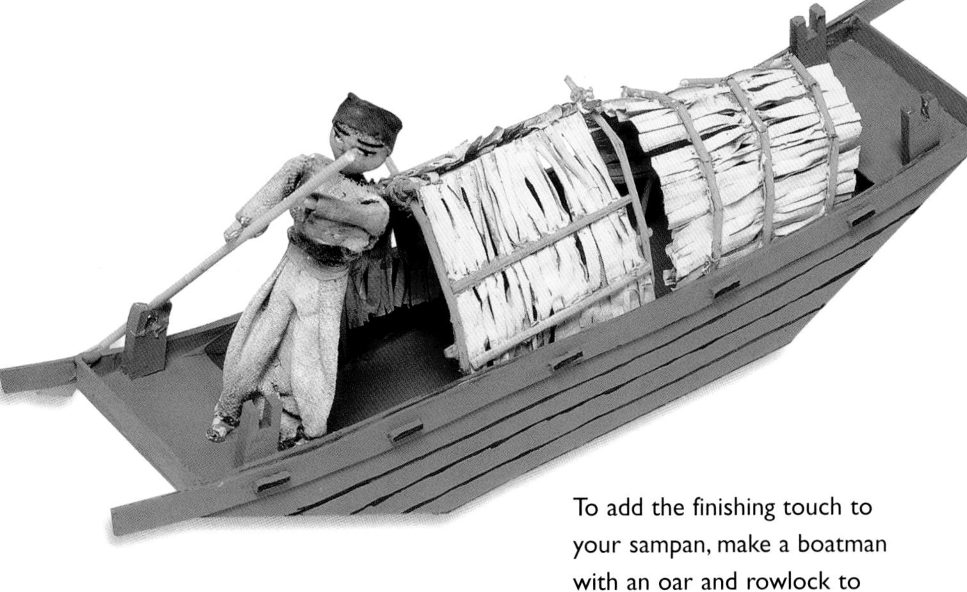

To add the finishing touch to your sampan, make a boatman with an oar and rowlock to propel the vessel.

Native American canoe

Many tribes native to North America were nomadic. At first, walking was their only form of transport across the land. Hunting and trade were the main reasons for travelling. Infants were carried in cradleboards, while Inuit babies in the Arctic were put into the hoods of their mothers' parkas. Carrying frames called travois were popular among those living on the Plains. Dogs dragged these frames at first, but horses replaced them in the late 1600s. Tribes could then travel greater distances to fresh hunting grounds.

Much of North America is covered with rivers, streams and lakes, and tribespeople were also skilled boatbuilders. There were bark canoes in the woodlands, large cedar canoes on the Northwest Coast and kayaks in the Arctic.

Templates

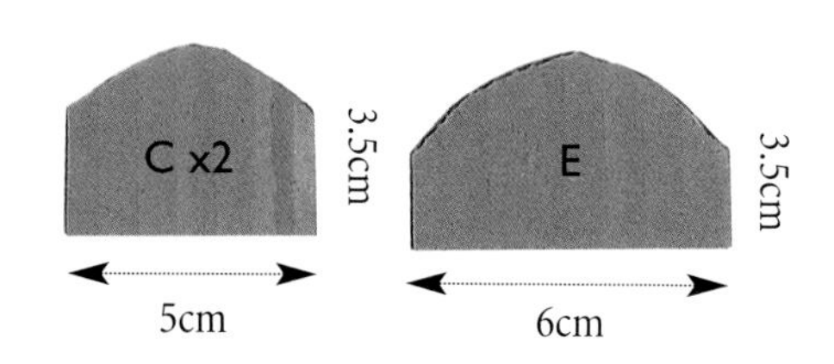

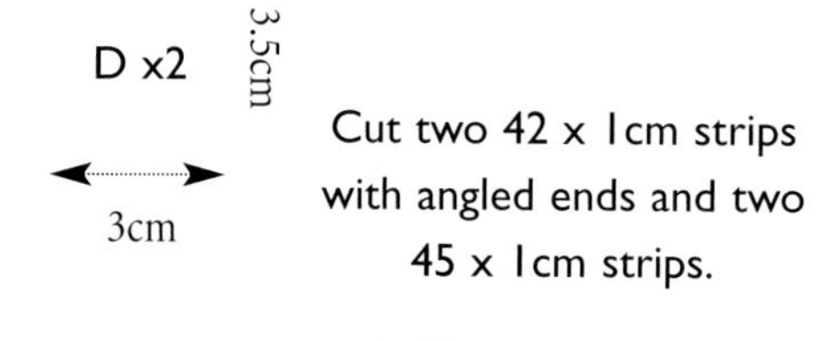

Cut two 42 x 1cm strips with angled ends and two 45 x 1cm strips.

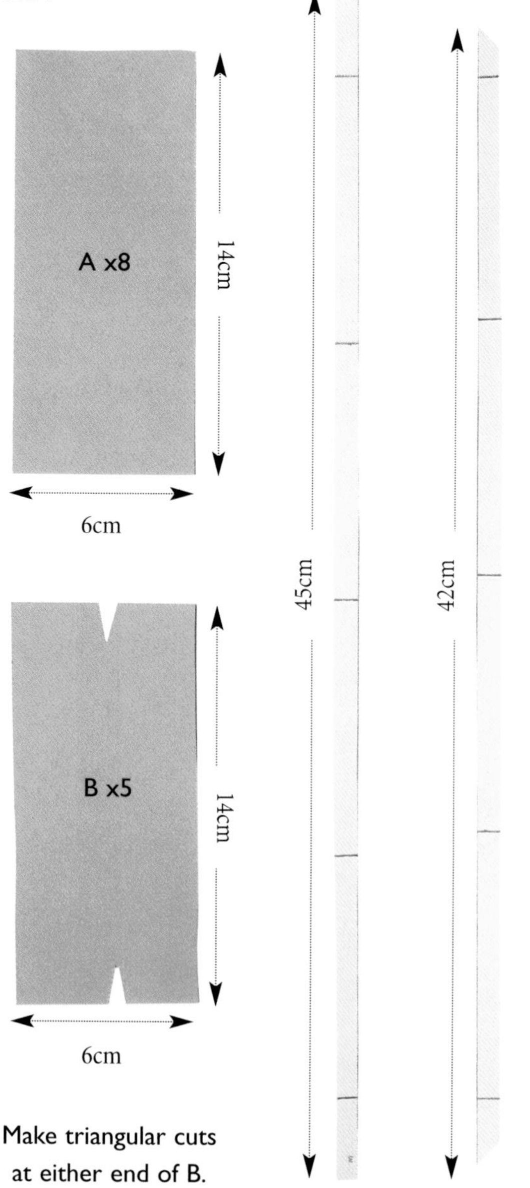

Make triangular cuts at either end of B.

▲ Into America
The first Native Americans probably came from Siberia. They crossed land bridges at the Bering Strait around 13,000BC.

YOU WILL NEED

Thick card (templates C, D and E), brown paper (templates A and B), cream paper (strips), pencil, ruler, scissors, PVA glue and glue brush, needle and thread, brown acrylic paints, paintbrush, water pot.

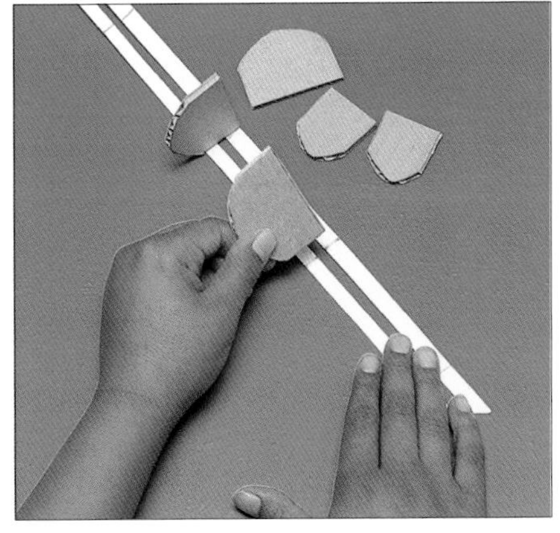

1 Cut out the templates. Starting at the centre, mark five evenly spaced lines on one 45cm strip and one 42cm strip. Glue the side of the E template across the centres of the strips.

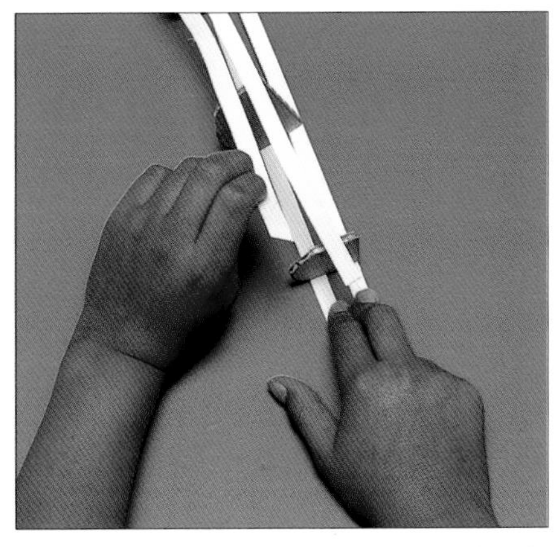

2 Glue the C template either side of the E template and the D templates either side of those. Line up the other two strips and glue those to the other sides of the C, D and E templates.

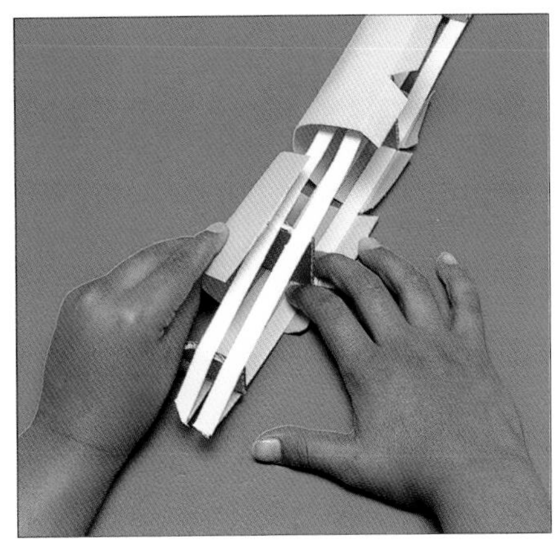

3 Glue the two 45cm strips and the two 42cm strips at both ends. Glue templates B to the frame, making sure that the cuts at either end fit over the C, D and E templates as shown.

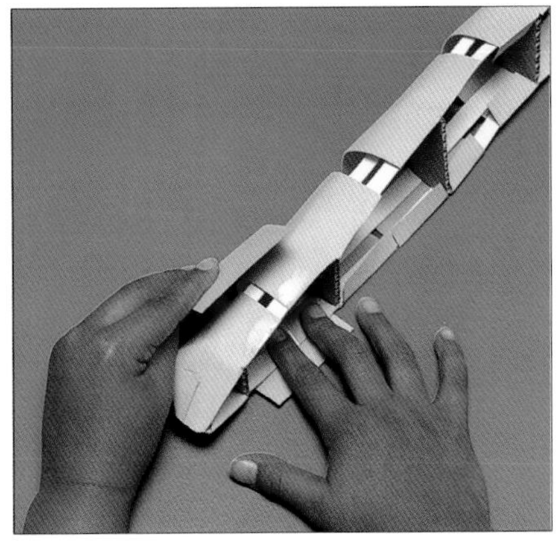

4 Tidy up the ends by gluing the excess paper around the frame of the canoe. Place four A templates over the gaps, and glue them to the top of the frame as shown above.

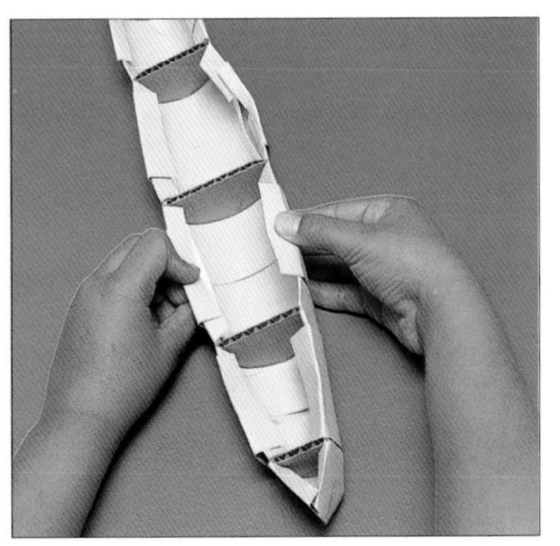

5 Stick the remaining A templates over the inside of the boat until the entire frame is covered. Carefully fold over and glue the tops of the paper around the top edge of the boat.

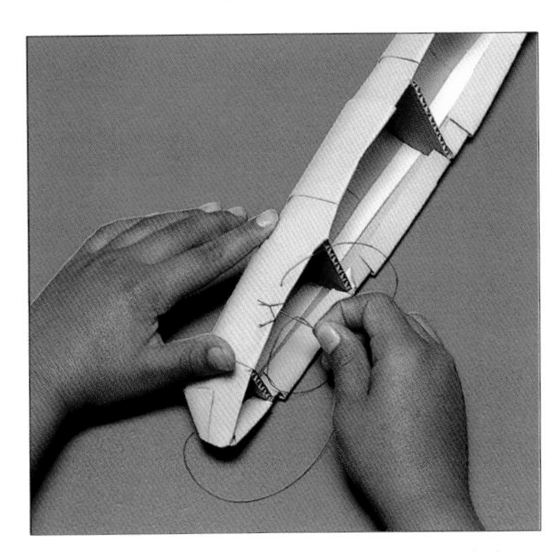

6 Thread the needle. Sew around the top edge of the boat to secure the flaps. Paint your boat brown and add detail. Make two paddles from thick card and paint them dark brown.

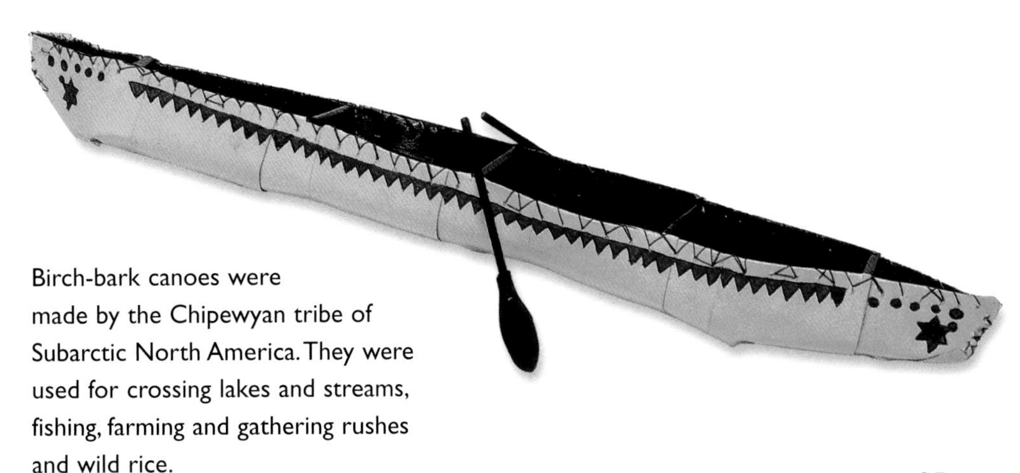

Birch-bark canoes were made by the Chipewyan tribe of Subarctic North America. They were used for crossing lakes and streams, fishing, farming and gathering rushes and wild rice.

Viking longship

The Vikings were excellent seafarers and were among the most skilful shipbuilders the world has ever seen. One of the most famous Viking vessels was the longship. It could be up to 23m in length. This long sailing ship was used for ocean voyages and warfare, and it was shallow enough to row up a river. The longship had an open deck without cabins or benches. The rowers sat on hide-covered sea chests that contained their possessions, weapons and food rations.

YOU WILL NEED

Thick card, balsa wood strips and pole, pale and dark brown paper, plain paper, pencil, ruler, scissors, craft knife, acrylic paints (black, brown and red), paintbrush, water pot, PVA glue and glue brush, masking tape, string.

Templates

Ask an adult to cut out the card and balsa wood templates following the measurements shown.

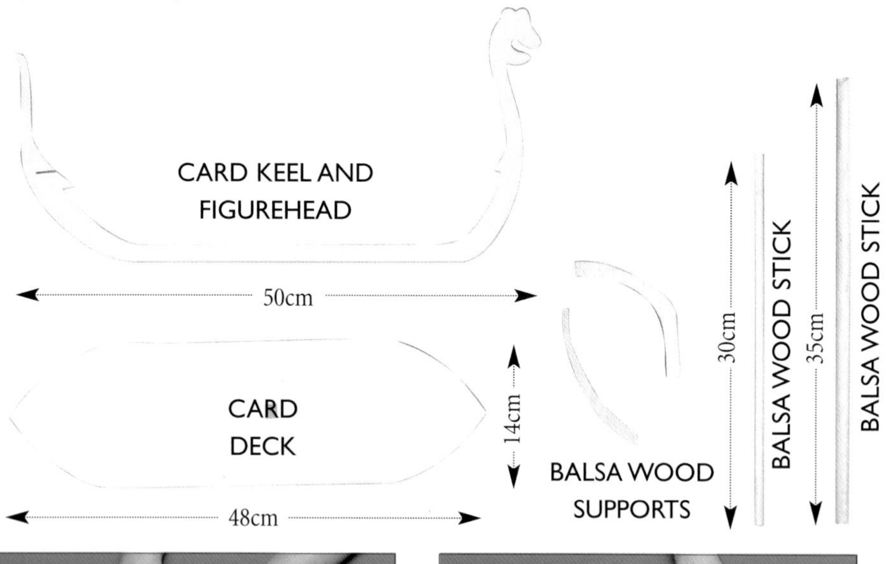

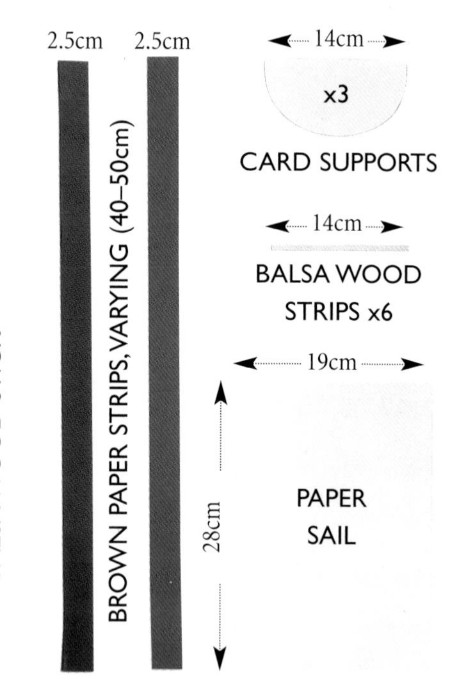

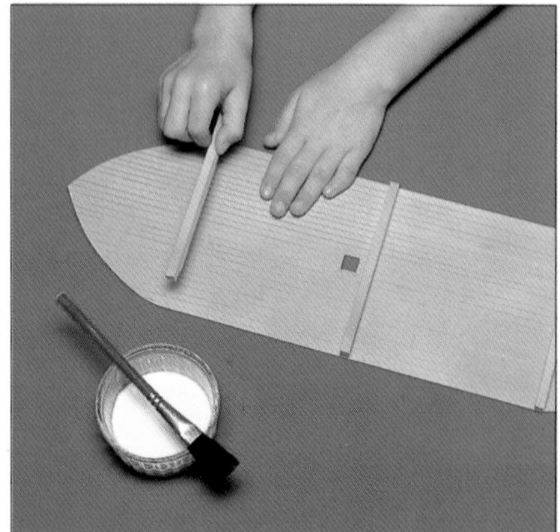

1 Paint the deck shape black on one side and brown on the other. Use a pencil to mark planks 5mm apart on the brown deck. Pierce a hole for the mast. Glue on three of the 14cm balsa strips.

2 Glue three 14cm balsa wood strips to the other side of the deck as in step 1, matching them with the planks on the other side. Then glue on the three card supports as crossbeams.

3 Carefully paint one side of the keel and figurehead template using bright red acrylic paint. Leave it to dry, turn it over and paint the other side of the card using the same colour.

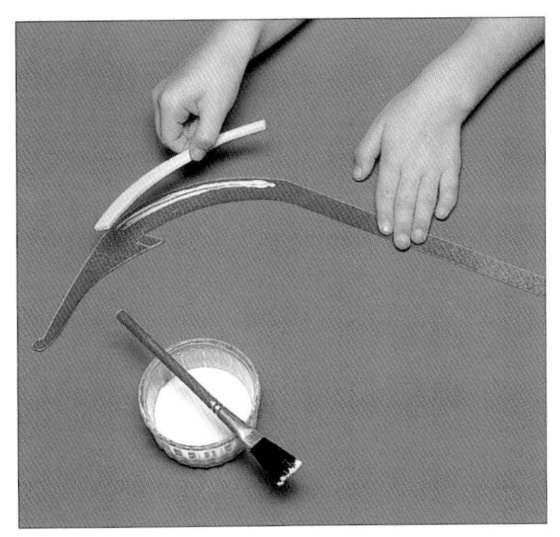

4 When the paint is completely dry, glue the two balsa wood supports either side of the curved parts of the keel as shown. These will strengthen the keel and figurehead section.

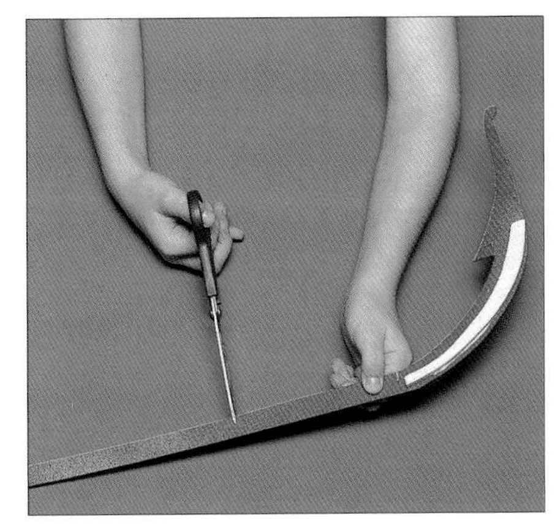

5 When the glue is dry, make three marks along the length of the keel, each one at a point that matches up to the crossbeams of the deck section. Use scissors to cut slots as shown.

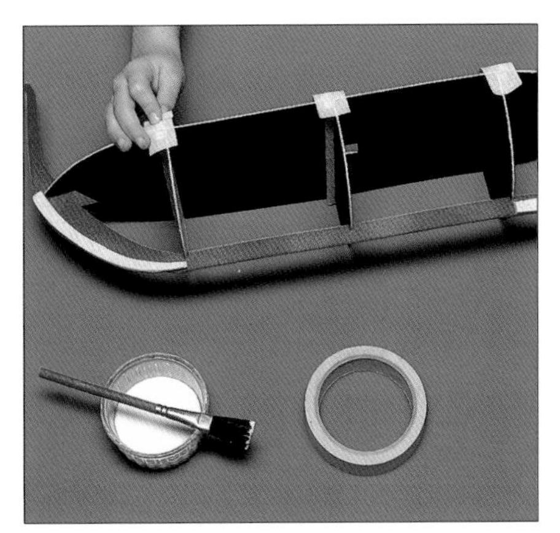

6 Slide the deck crossbeams into position on the keel slots and glue them in place. Use masking tape to make sure the joins are firm while the glue is drying.

7 Use varying lengths of pale and dark brown paper strips for the planks, or 'strakes', along each side of the keel. Carefully glue each strip into position along each side.

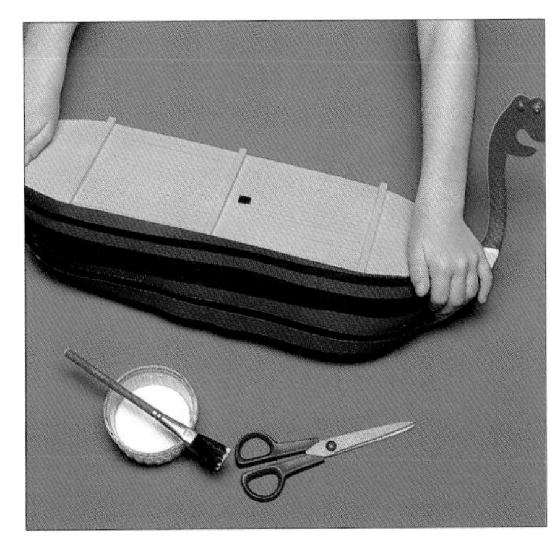

8 Continue gluing the strips into place. Alternate pale and dark brown strips to finish. Trim the excess off each strip as they get lower so that they form a curve.

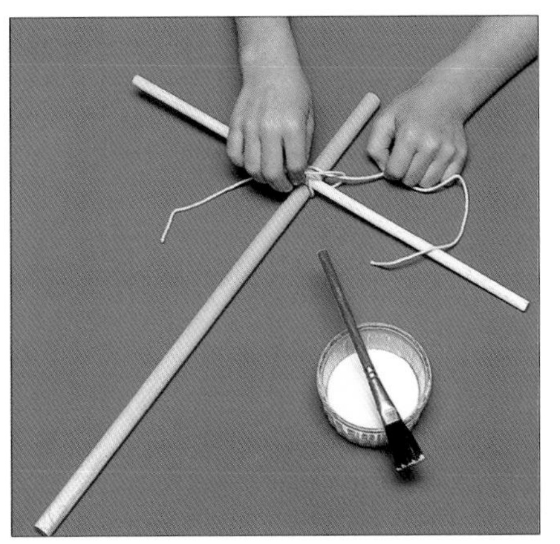

9 Make a mast using the 30cm long balsa wood and the 35cm long stick. Glue the two pieces firmly together and bind them with string as shown above.

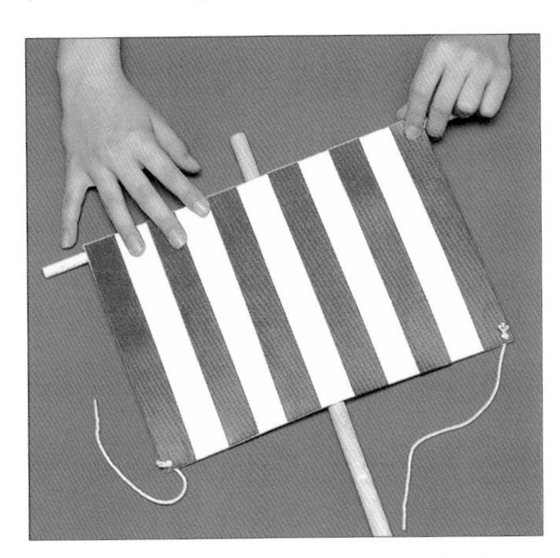

10 Paint the sail with red and white stripes. Glue the sail to the 30cm cross beam. Attach string as rigging at the bottom of the sail. Add card eyes to the dragon on the figurehead.

A longship put to sea with a crew of around 30 fighting men. Each one knew how to fight as well as how to man the oars. The round shields of the warriors were slotted along the side of the ship. An awning of sailcloth could be erected to keep off the sun or rain.

Celtic wagon

After around 200BC, the Celts began to build fortified settlements as centres of government, craftwork and trade. Some grew up around existing hill forts or villages; others occupied fresh sites. The Romans called them *oppida* (towns). Some of the oppida were very large. For example, Manching, in southern Germany, covered about 380ha, and its protective walls were over 7km long.

Travel between the settlements was slow and difficult compared with today. There were no paved roads, although the Celts did build causeways of wood across marshy ground. Overland journeys were on foot or horseback, and only the wealthiest chieftains could afford to drive a chariot. The Celts used wooden carts pulled by oxen to transport heavy loads of farm produce, timber or salt. Oxen were very valuable and were the main source of wealth for many farmers.

YOU WILL NEED

White card, pencil, ruler, scissors, felt-tipped pen, PVA glue and glue brush, balsa wood, masking tape, sandpaper, pair of compasses, drawing pins, leather thong, silver paint, paintbrush, water pot.

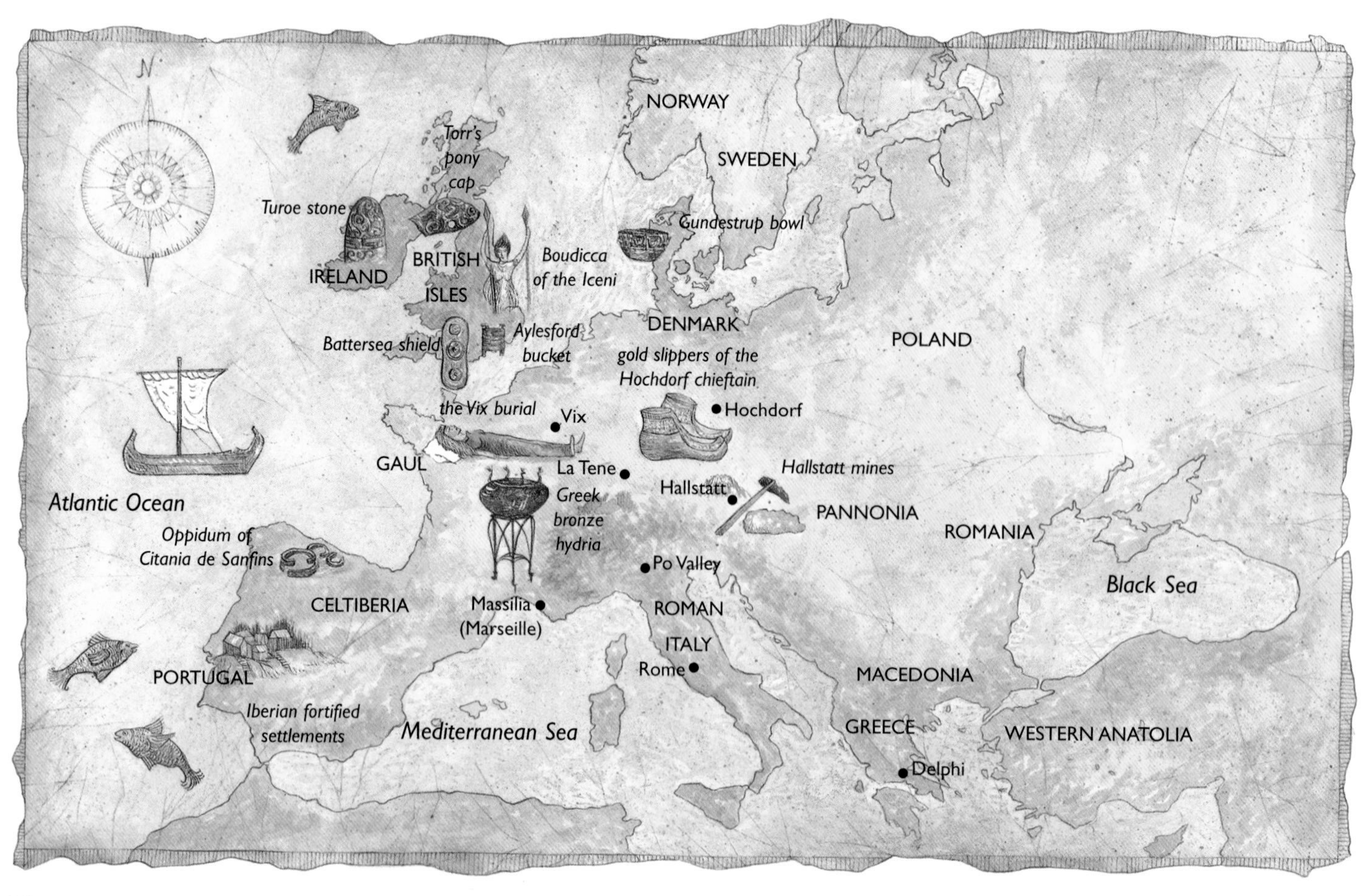

▾ Linking up
European trade routes followed great river valleys or connected small ports along the coast, from Ireland to Portugal. The Celts spread far and wide and, by 200BC, had even attacked and defeated the Romans in various parts of Europe and had attacked Greece's holy temple of Apollo at Delphi.

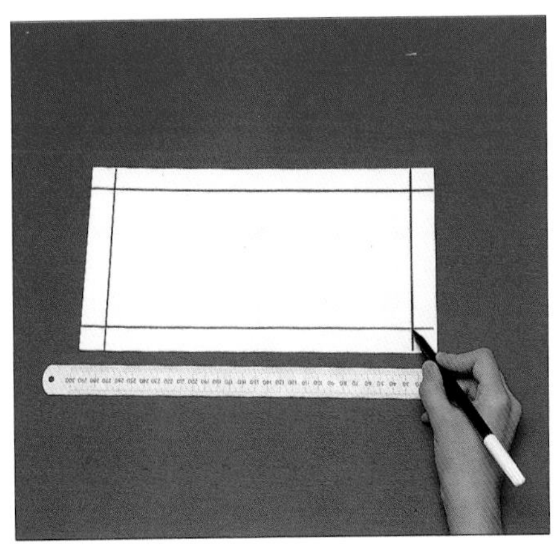

1 Measure and cut out a piece of white card to 29 x 16cm. Using a ruler and felt-tipped pen, draw lines to make a border 2cm in from the edges of the card as shown above.

2 Make cuts in the corners of the card as shown above. Score along each line and then fold the edges up to make a box shape. This will be the body of the wagon.

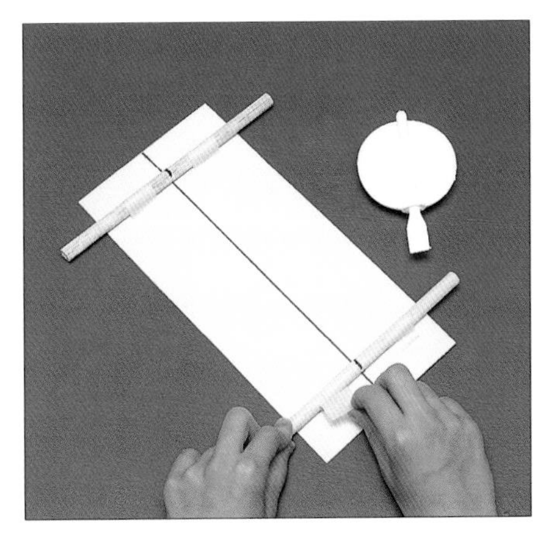

3 Measure and cut out another piece of card to 27 x 12cm. Take two lengths of balsa wood, each measuring 20cm. Glue and tape the balsa across the card 4cm in from the two ends.

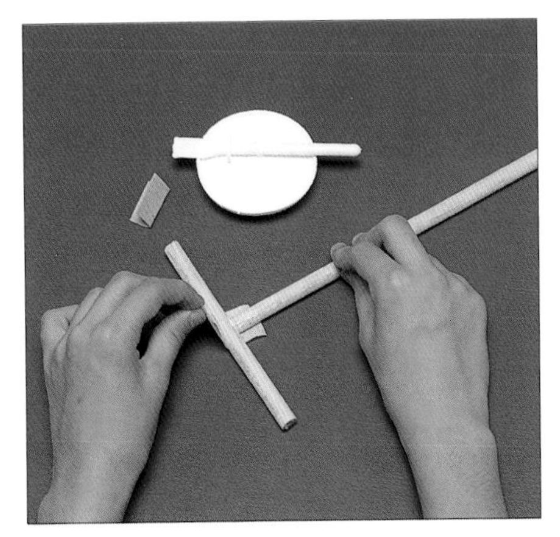

4 Take two sticks of balsa , one 26cm in length and the other 11cm. Sand the end of the long stick to fit against the shorter piece. Glue the pieces together. Secure with tape until dry.

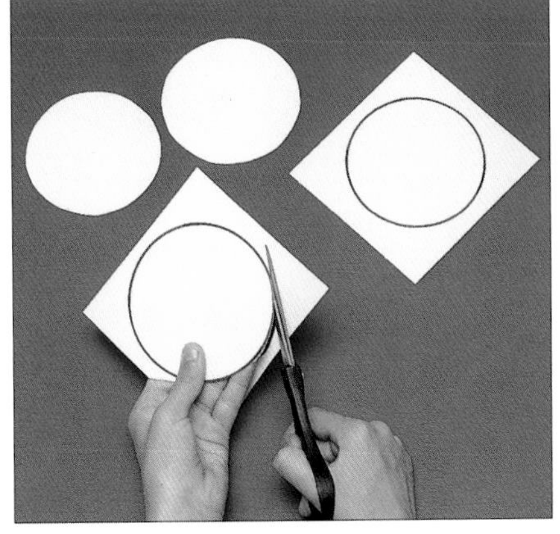

5 Use the compasses to draw four circles on four pieces of card, each measuring 10cm in diameter. Then carefully cut the circles out as shown above.

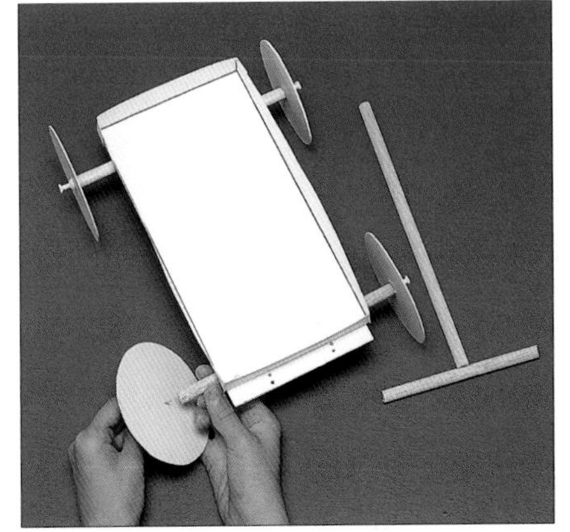

6 Glue the wagon body on to the card with balsa attached. Fix the wheels to the balsa wood shafts by pressing a drawing pin through the centre of each wheel.

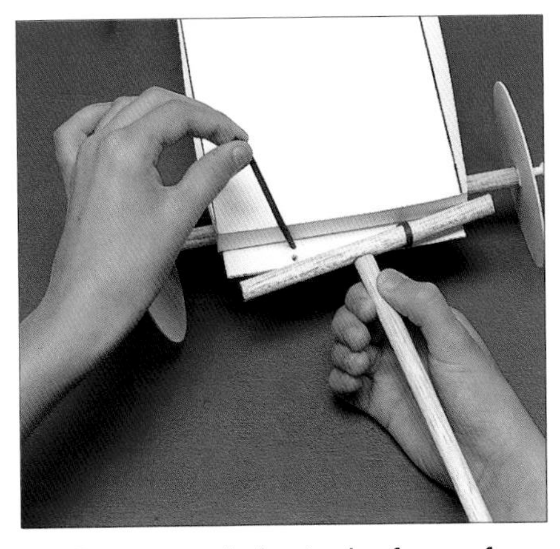

7 Pierce two holes in the front of the wagon. Thread the leather thong through the holes and tie it to the T-shaped steering pole you made in step 4. Paint the wagon silver.

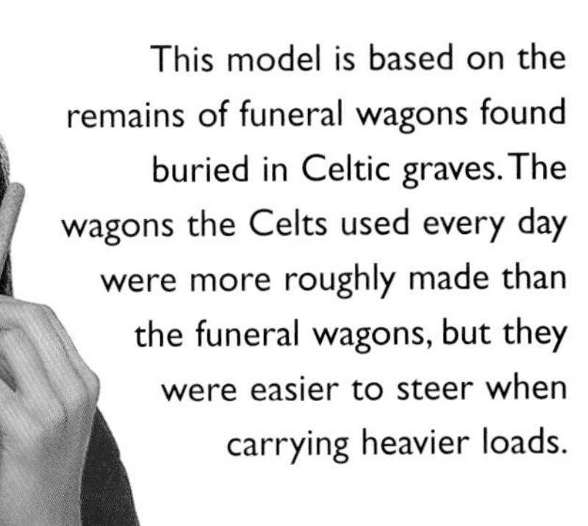

This model is based on the remains of funeral wagons found buried in Celtic graves. The wagons the Celts used every day were more roughly made than the funeral wagons, but they were easier to steer when carrying heavier loads.

Arctic sledge

The surface of the Arctic Ocean is partially frozen throughout the year and in winter snow covers the land. In the past, sledges were the most common way of travelling over ice and snow. They were made from bone or timber and lashed together with strips of animal hide or whale sinew. They glided over the snow on runners made from walrus tusks or wood. Arctic sledges had to be light enough to be pulled by animals, yet strong enough to carry an entire family and its belongings. In North America, the Inuit used huskies to pull their sledges. In Siberia and Scandinavia, however, reindeer were used to pull sledges. In ancient times, Arctic peoples often used skis to get around. They were made of wood and the undersides were covered with strips of reindeer skin. The hairs on the skin pointed backwards, allowing the skier to climb up hills.

▲ Getting around
Today, petrol-driven snowmobiles make for quick and easy travel across the Arctic ice. In the past, Arctic people relied on animals to pull sledges across the frozen landscape.

YOU WILL NEED
Thick card, balsa wood, ruler, pencil, scissors, craft knife, PVA glue and glue brush, masking tape, pair of compasses, barbecue stick, brown acrylic paint, paintbrush, water pot, string, chamois leather, card box.

▼ Travelling companions
Huskies are well adapted to life in the harsh Arctic cold. Their thick coats keep the animals warm in bitterly cold temperatures as low as –50°C, and they can sleep peacefully in the fiercest of blizzards. The snow builds up against their fur and insulates them.

Templates

A RUNNERS x4

6.5cm

54cm

Draw the shapes on card (use balsa wood for template C) and cut them out. Glue two A templates together. Repeat this for the other two A templates. Do the same for all four B templates. Cover all the edges with masking tape.

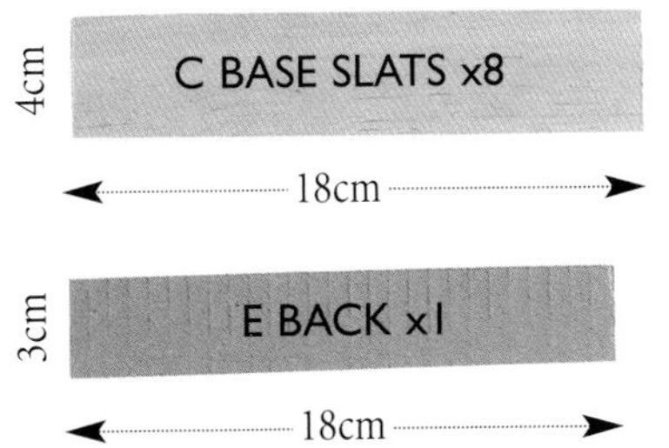

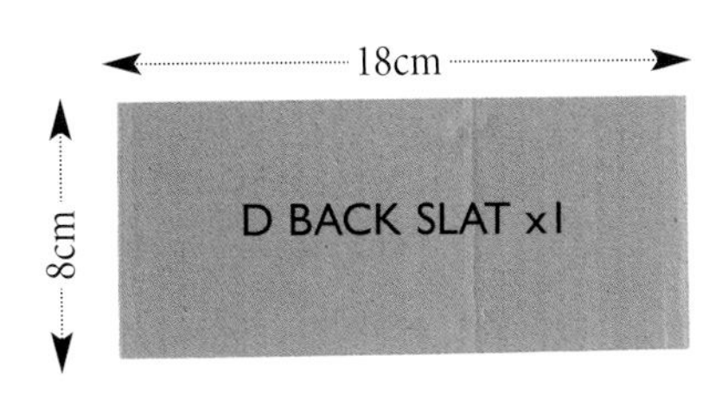

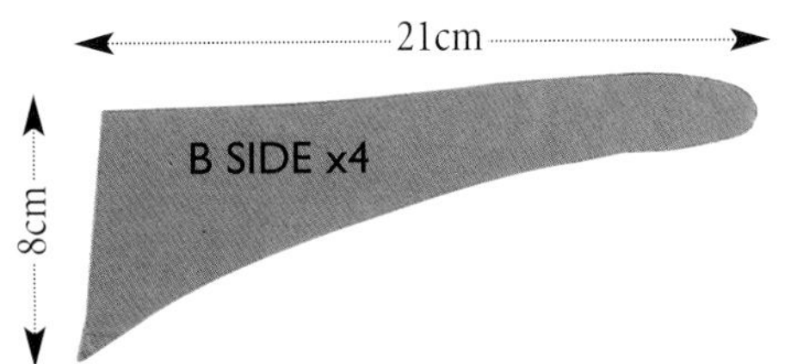

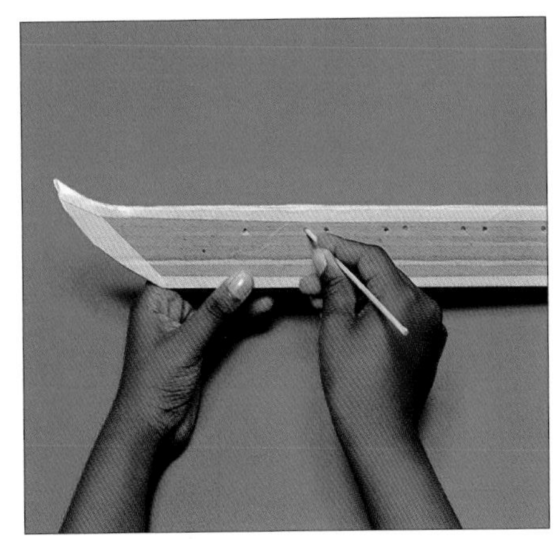

1 Using a small pair of compasses, make small holes along the top edge of the glued A templates. Use the end of a barbecue stick to make the holes a little larger.

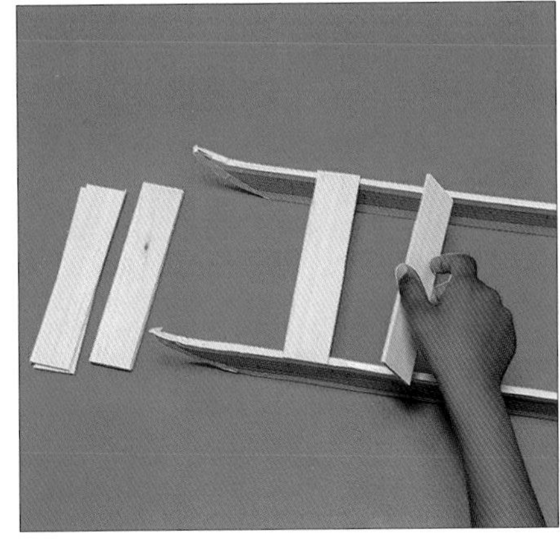

2 Glue the balsa wood slats C in position over the holes along the A templates as shown above. You will need to use all eight balsa wood slats. Glue back slat D in position.

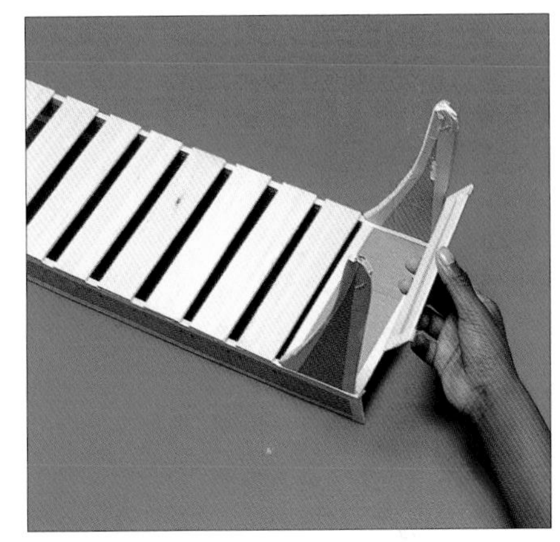

3 Carefully glue the B templates and the E template to the edge of the sledge as shown above. Allow the glue to dry completely before painting the model sledge.

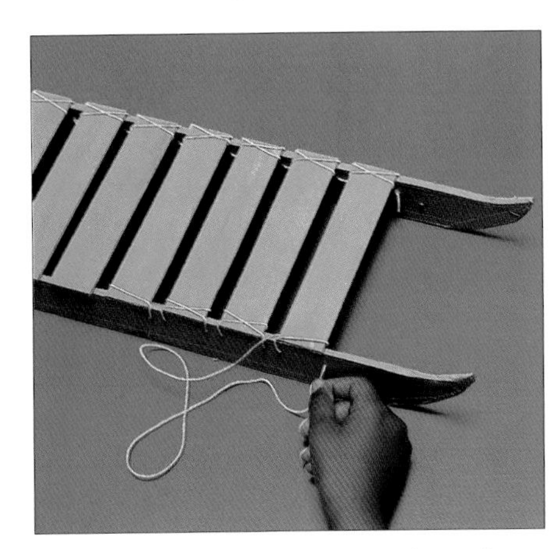

4 Thread lengths of string through the holes to secure the slats on each side. Decorate the sledge with a chamois-covered card box and secure it to the sledge.

Inuit hunters used wooden sledges pulled by huskies to hunt for food over a large area. The wood was lashed together with animal hide or sinew.

Military Technology

People have always needed to defend themselves or fight for more land. The development of weaponry runs alongside the growth of the earliest civilizations. Weapons were needed, not just for hunting, but for defence and attack. From the very beginning, there were two distinct types of weapon – missiles such as the spear, which could be thrown from a distance, and strike weapons such as the club, which could be used at close quarters. Stone Age people used sharpened flints for daggers and spears. As time passed, these early weapons were eventually replaced by steel swords, heavy artillery and pistols.

▲ War chariot

The Hittites controlled much of Anatolia (modern-day Turkey) and parts of Mesopotamia and Syria. Much of their military success came from their skill as charioteers. Hittite chariots held up to three people, one to drive the horses and two to fight. Hittite charioteers were feared by their enemies.

◀ Light cavalry

The horse of this Persian warrior is not protected by armour so it needs to be fast and nimble. The warrior carries only a short spear so that he can make a quick strike against the enemy and then retreat.

◂ Crow's beak

The Romans developed a grappling weapon called a corvus, which looked rather like a crow's big beak. (*Corvus* is the Latin word for crow.) It was a hinged gangplank with a spike that sank into the enemy ship's deck. Twin-hulled siege vessels carried fighting towers to the enemy.

◂ Warriors of Japan

Japanese warriors were called samurai. They fought with deadly, two-handed swords and were dressed in padded armour and helmets. The armour consisted of bamboo plates sewn on to a padded jacket. Mythical motifs decorated the helmet.

Top heavy ▸

This Asian soldier carries an array of different weapons – a sword, a dagger, bow and arrows, an axe and a shield. The sword was heavier at the tip, which gave it greater weight when he swung it down on his enemy.

Greek sword and shield

When the Greeks went to war, it was usually to engage in raids and sieges of rival city states. Major battles with foreign powers were rare, but the results could be devastating. Army commanders chose their ground with care and relied heavily on the discipline and training of their troops. The core of a Greek army consisted of foot soldiers called hoplites. Their strength as a fighting force lay in their bristling spears, singled-edged swords, overlapping shields and sheer weight of numbers.

YOU WILL NEED

String, pencil, pair of compasses, ruler, thick card, scissors, PVA glue and glue brush, gold paper, silver paper, masking tape, black acrylic paint, paintbrush, water pot, aluminium foil.

1 Tie a 22cm length of string to a pencil and compasses. Draw a circle on to the card as shown above. Carefully cut around the edge of the circle using your scissors.

2 Make a cut into the centre of the circle as shown above. Line the edges of the cut with glue. Overlap the edges by 2cm, and stick them together so that your shield is slightly curved.

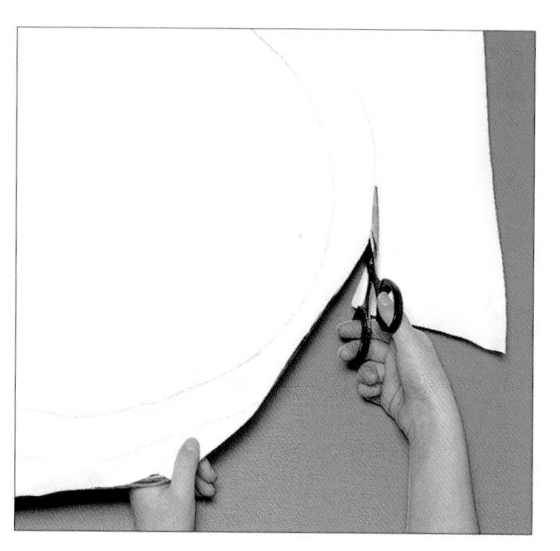

3 Place the card circle on to a piece of gold paper and draw around it. Draw another circle 2cm larger than the first. Cut out the larger gold circle as shown above.

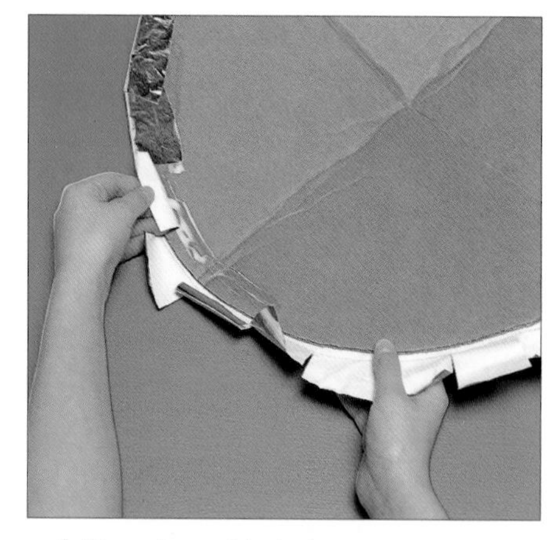

4 Glue the gold circle on to your card circle. Make small cuts along the edges of the gold paper. Fold the edges over the circle and glue them to the back of the card circle.

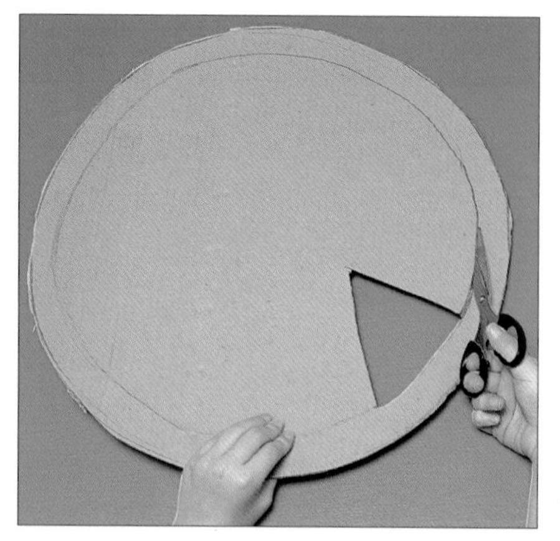

5 Use the string and compasses to draw another 22cm circle on to a piece of card. Draw another circle 2cm smaller than the first. Cut out the inner circle in stages with scissors.

6 Cut through the ring of card in one place as shown above. Cover the ring with silver paper. Wrap the silver paper around the card and glue it down securely.

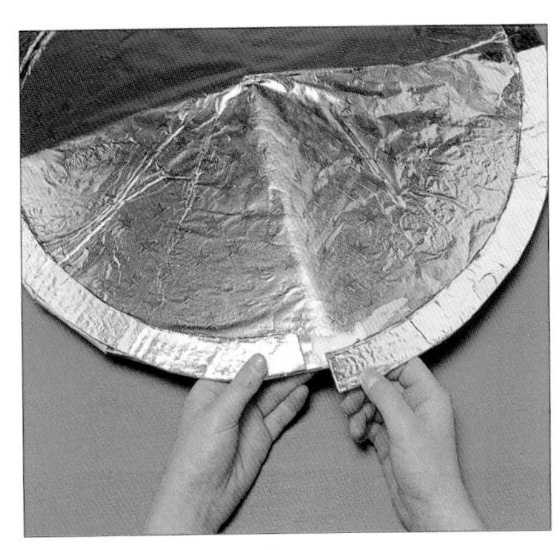

7 Glue the silver ring around the edge of the gold shield as shown above. You will have to overlap the ends of the silver disc to fit it neatly around the shield.

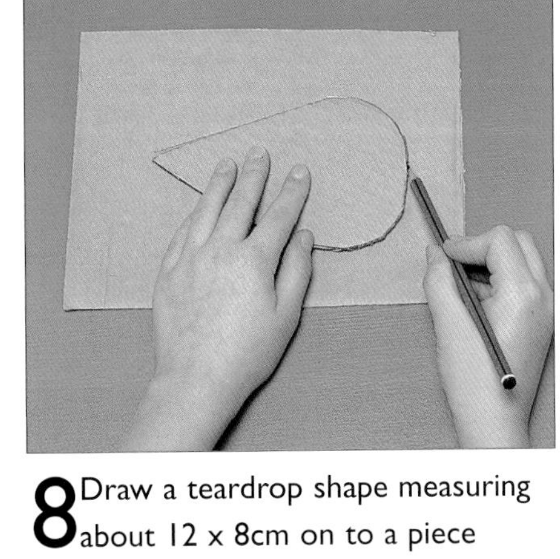

8 Draw a teardrop shape measuring about 12 x 8cm on to a piece of thick card. Cut the teardrop shape out. Make four more teardrops using the first one as a template.

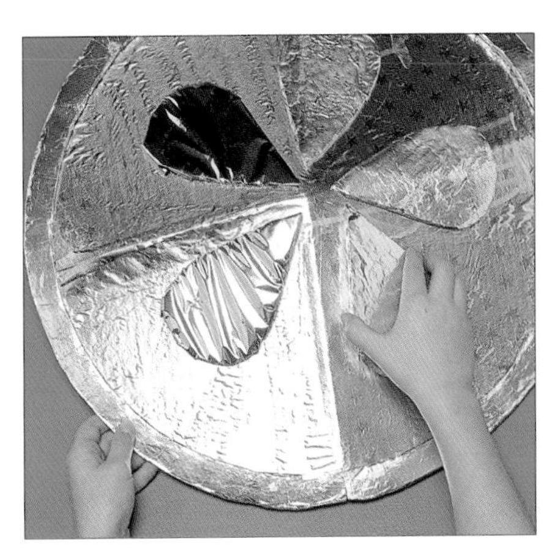

9 Cover and glue silver paper to three teardrops and gold paper to two teardrops. Then glue the teardrops on to the gold shield, keeping them evenly spaced, as shown above.

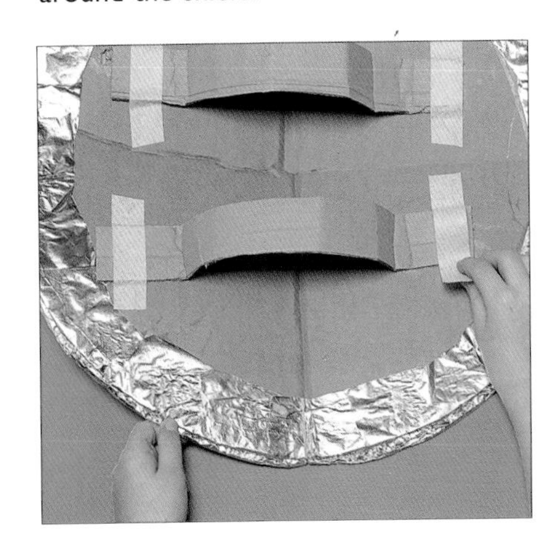

10 Cut out two strips of card 25 x 3cm. Curve the strips. Glue them on to the back of the shield to make a pair of handles big enough for your arm to fit through. Secure with masking tape.

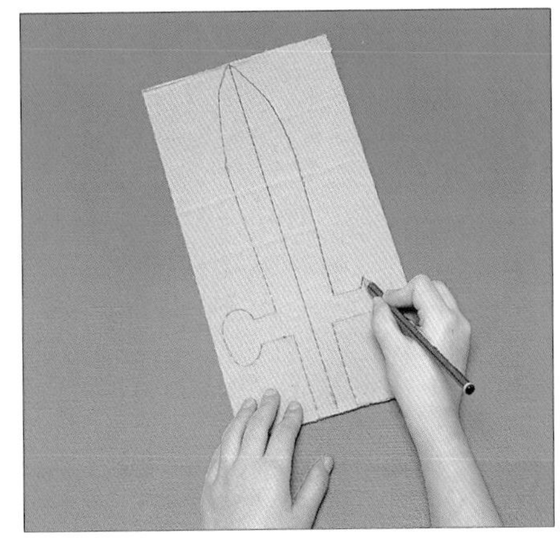

11 Cut out a rectangle of thick card measuring 30 x 15cm. Draw a line down the centre of the card as a guide. Draw a sword shape on to the card.

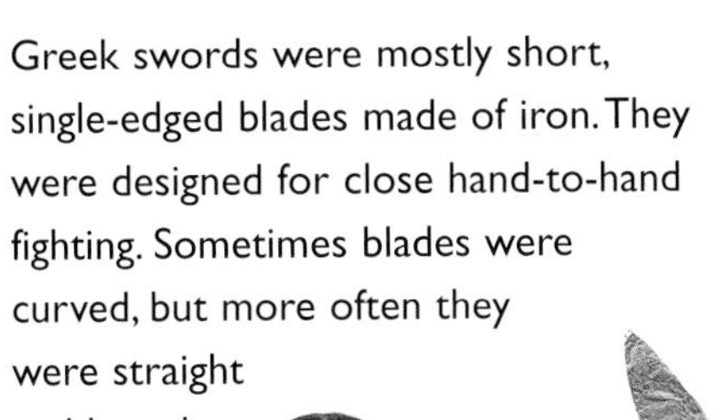

Greek swords were mostly short, single-edged blades made of iron. They were designed for close hand-to-hand fighting. Sometimes blades were curved, but more often they were straight and broad.

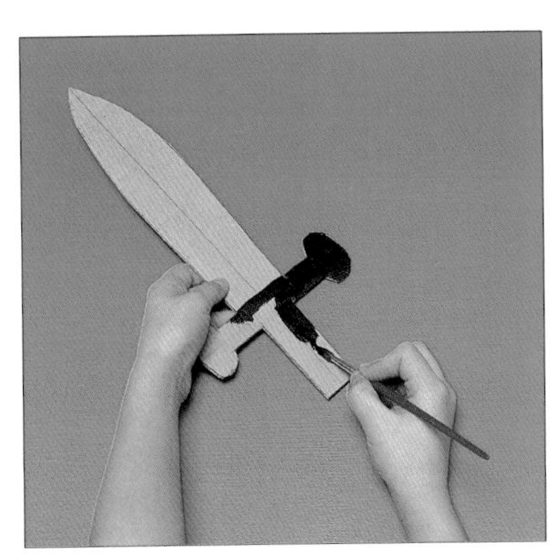

12 Cut out the sword shape from the card. Paint one side of the handle with black paint. When the paint is dry, turn the sword over and paint the other side of the handle.

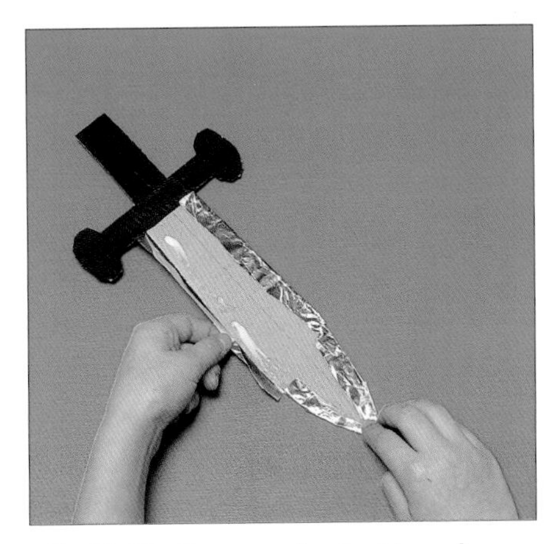

13 Finally, cover both sides of the blade of the sword with aluminium foil and neatly glue it down. The aluminium foil will give the blade of your sword a shiny surface.

Greek warrior greaves

Greek men of fighting age were expected to swear allegiance to the army of the city in which they lived. In Sparta, the army was on duty all year round. In other parts of Greece, men gave up fighting in autumn to bring in the harvest and make wine. The only full-time soldiers in these states were the personal bodyguards of a ruler or mercenaries who fought for anyone who paid them.

Armies consisted mainly of hoplites (foot soldiers) and cavalry (soldiers on horseback). The cavalry was less effective in war because the riders had no stirrups. The cavalry was mainly used for scouting, harassing a beaten enemy and carrying messages. The hoplites, who engaged in hand-to-hand combat, were the most important fighting force. The hoplites' armour consisted of a shield, helmet, spear, sword and metal shin protectors called greaves.

▲ Raw materials
Tin and copper were smelted to make bronze, the main material for Greek weaponry and armour. Bronze is harder than pure copper and, unlike iron, does not rust. As there was no tin in Greece, it was imported.

◀ Show of strength
The fighting force known as the hoplites was made up of middle-class men who could afford the weapons. The body of a hoplite soldier was protected by a bronze cuirass (a one-piece breast- and backplate). The cuirass was worn over a leather tunic. Their bronze helmets were often crested with horsehair. Shields were usually round and decorated with a symbol.

YOU WILL NEED

Clear film, plaster bandages, bowl of water, sheet of paper, kitchen paper, scissors, cord, gold paint, paintbrush, water pot.

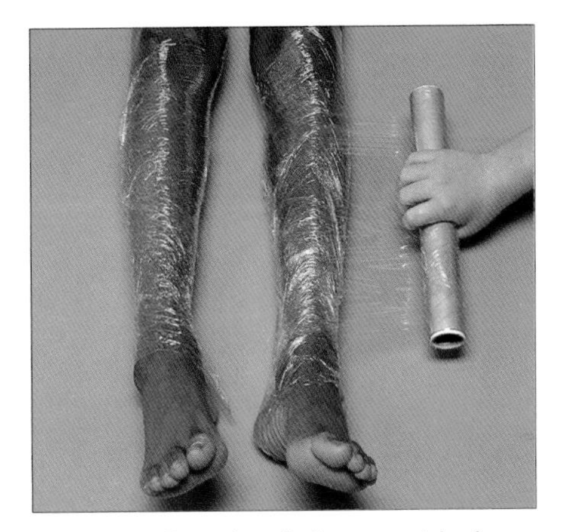

1 Ask a friend to help you with the first three steps. Loosely cover both of your legs (from your ankle to the top of your knee) in clear film as shown above.

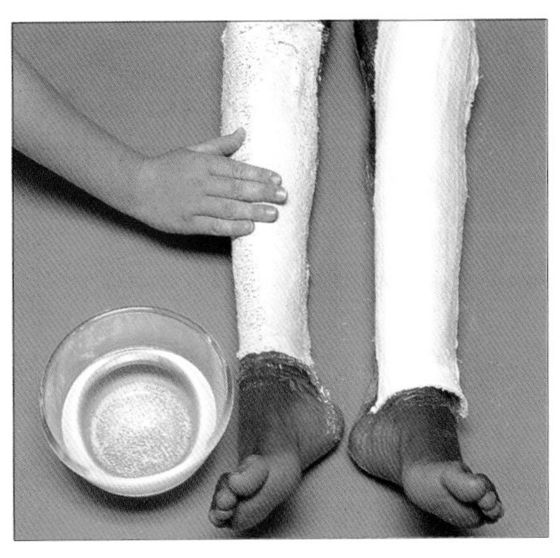

2 Soak each plaster bandage in water. Working from one side of your leg to another, smooth the bandage over the front of your leg. You will need to use several layers of plaster bandage.

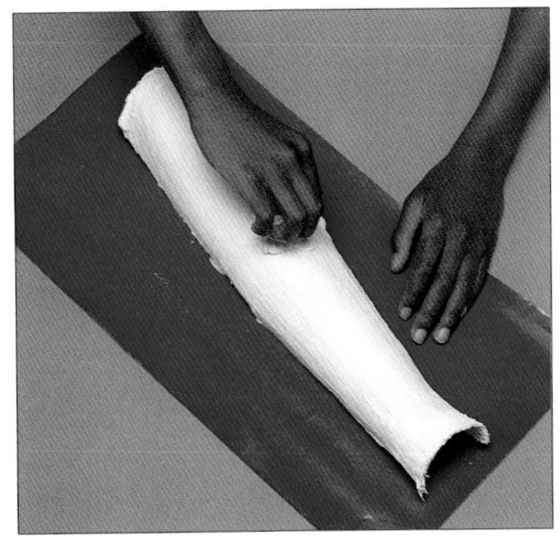

3 When you have finished, carefully remove each greave. Set them out on a sheet of paper. Dampen some kitchen paper and use it to smooth the greaves down. Let them dry.

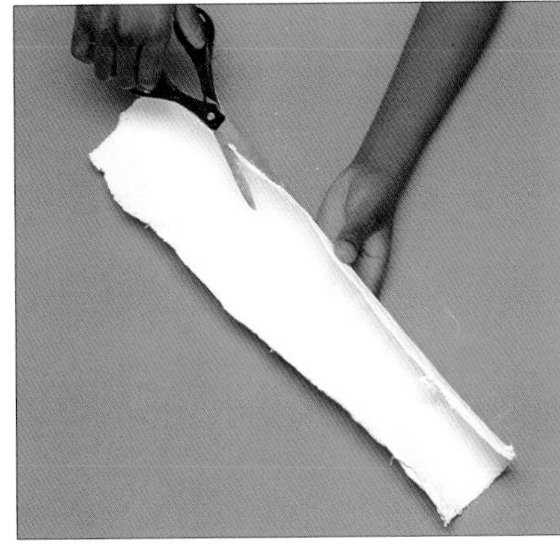

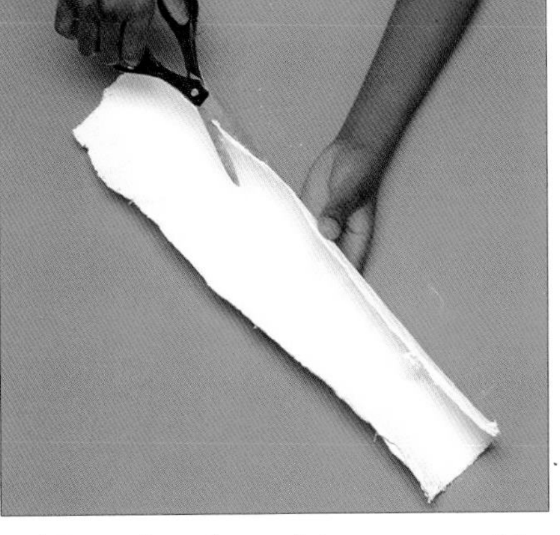

4 Trim the edges of the greaves with scissors to make them look neat. Measure four lengths of cord to fit around your legs – one below each knee and one above each ankle.

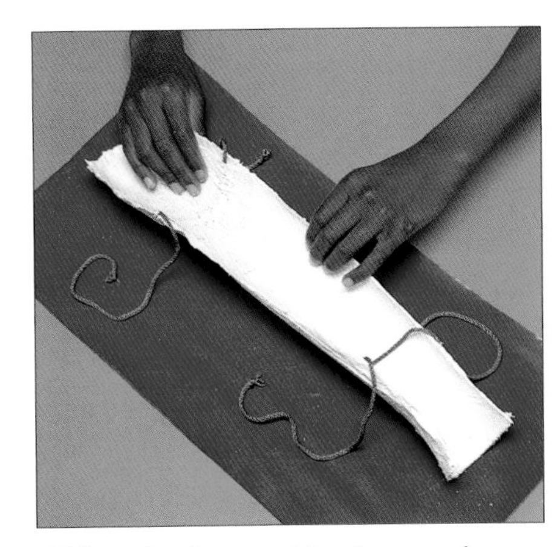

5 Lay the first cord in place on the back of the greaves where you want to tie them to your legs. Fix the cord in place with more wet plaster bandages. Repeat with the other three cords.

6 Let the plaster bandages dry with the cord in place. Now paint each greave with a layer of gold paint. Once they are dry, tie the greaves around your legs.

Greaves were attached to the lower legs to protect them in battle. Real greaves were made of bronze and would have been very heavy.

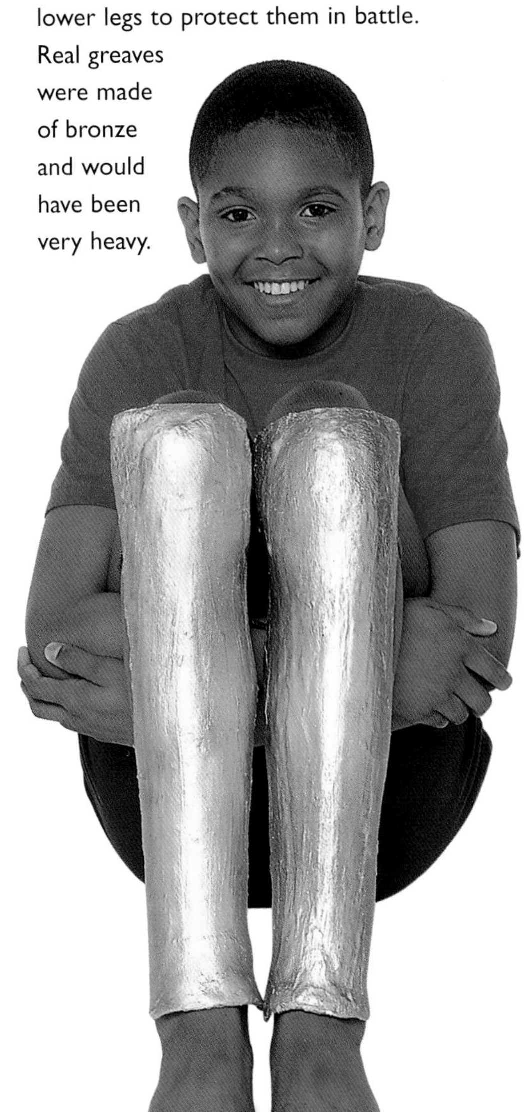

Roman armour

Soldiers in the Roman Empire were well equipped for fighting. A legionary was armed with a *pugio* (dagger) and a *gladius* (short iron sword) for stabbing and slashing. He also carried a *pilum* (javelin) of iron and wood. In the early days, a foot soldier's armour was a mail shirt, worn over a short, thick tunic. Officers wore a cuirass – a bronze casing that protected the chest and back. By about AD35, plate armour replaced the mail shirt. The iron plates (sections) were joined by hooks or leather straps. Early shields were oval, and later ones were oblong with curved edges. They were made of layers of wood glued together, covered in leather and linen. A metal boss over the central handle could be used to hit an enemy who got too close.

▲ Overseas duty
Roman soldiers were recruited from all parts of the enormous empire, including Africa. They were often sent on duty far away from their home. This was to make sure they did not desert.

▲ Highlight of the games
The chariot was not used a great deal by the Roman army. However, it was a popular sight at the public games held in Rome and other major cities. Most chariots held two people. If there was only one rider, he would tie the reins around his waist. This kept his hands free so he could use his weapons.

YOU WILL NEED

Tape measure, A1 sheets of metal-coloured card (one or two, depending on how big you are), pencil, scissors, PVA glue and glue brush, 2m length of cord, pair of compasses.

1 Measure the size of your chest. Cut out three strips of card, 5cm wide and long enough to fit around your chest. Cut out some thinner strips to stick the three main ones together.

2 Lay the wide strips flat and glue them together with the thin strips you cut. Let the glue dry. The Romans would have used leather straps to hold the wide metal pieces together.

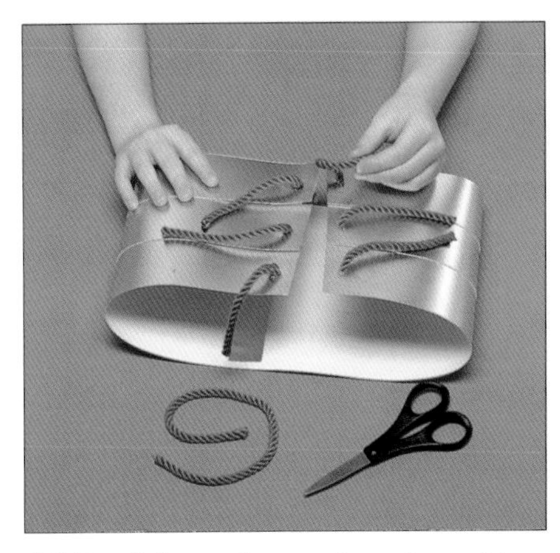

3 Bend the ends together, silver side out. Pierce a hole in the end of each strip using scissors. Cut 6 pieces of cord and pull through, knotting the cord at the back.

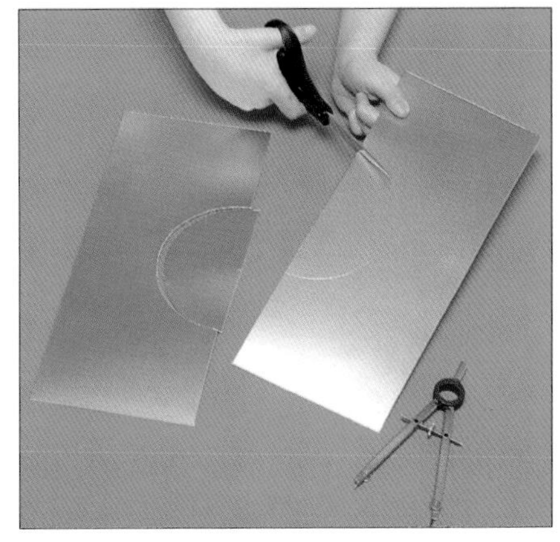

4 Cut a square of card as wide as your shoulders. Use a pair of compasses to draw a 12cm-diameter circle in the centre. Cut the square in half and cut away the half circles.

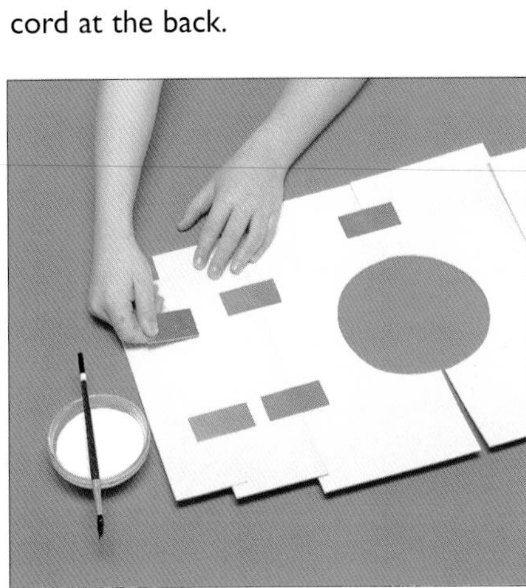

5 Use smaller strips of card to glue the shoulder halves together but leaving a neck hole. Cut out four more strips, two a little shorter than the others. Attach them in the same way.

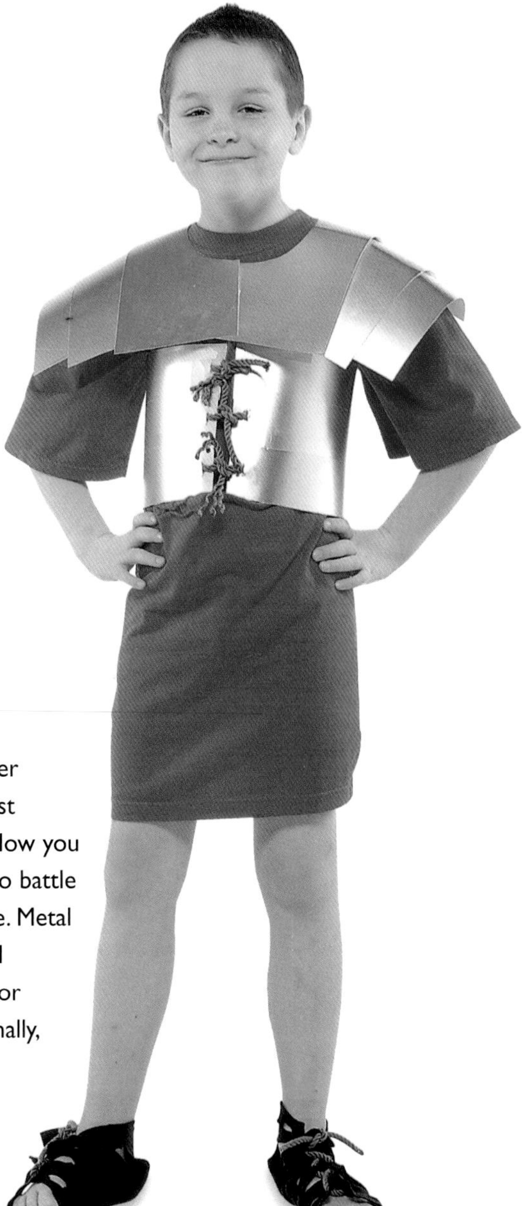

Put the shoulder piece over your head and tie the chest section around yourself. Now you are a legionary ready to do battle with the enemies of Rome. Metal strip armour was invented during the reign of Emperor Tiberius (AD 14–37). Originally, the various parts of metal strip armour were hinged and joined together either by hooks or by buckles and straps.

Japanese samurai helmet

During the Japanese civil wars, between 1185 and 1600, emperors, shoguns (governors) and daimyo (nobles) all relied on armies of samurai (warriors) to fight their battles. Samurai were skilled fighters. Members of each army were bound together by a solemn oath, sworn to their lord, who gave them rich rewards. The civil wars ended around 1600, when the Tokugawa Dynasty of shoguns came to power. After this time, samurai spent less time fighting, and served their lords as officials and business managers.

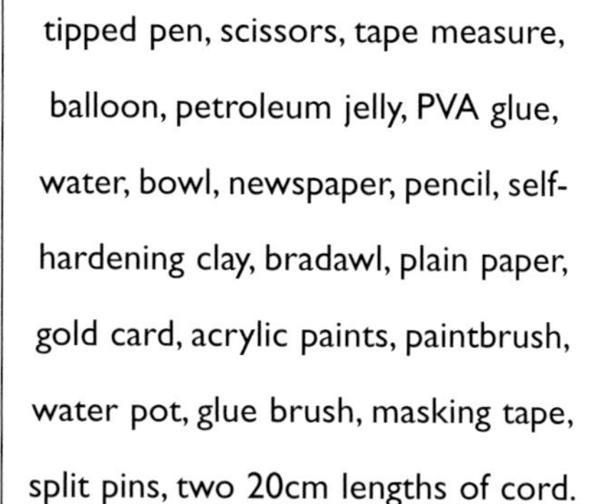

YOU WILL NEED

Thick card, pin, string, ruler, felt-tipped pen, scissors, tape measure, balloon, petroleum jelly, PVA glue, water, bowl, newspaper, pencil, self-hardening clay, bradawl, plain paper, gold card, acrylic paints, paintbrush, water pot, glue brush, masking tape, split pins, two 20cm lengths of cord.

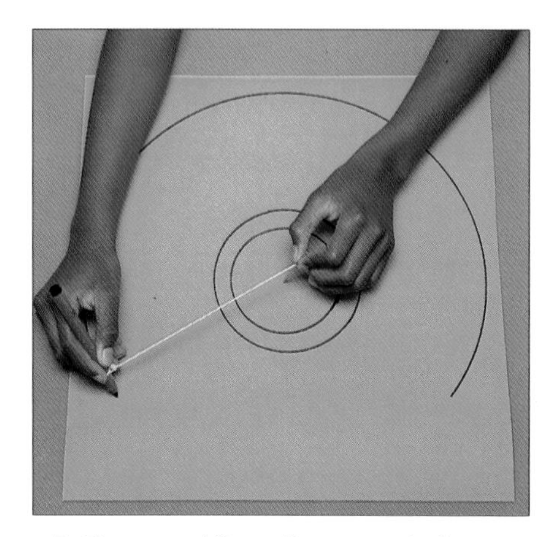

1 Draw an 18cm-diameter circle on to a piece of thick card using the pin, string and felt-tipped pen. Draw two larger circles 20cm and 50cm in diameter as shown above.

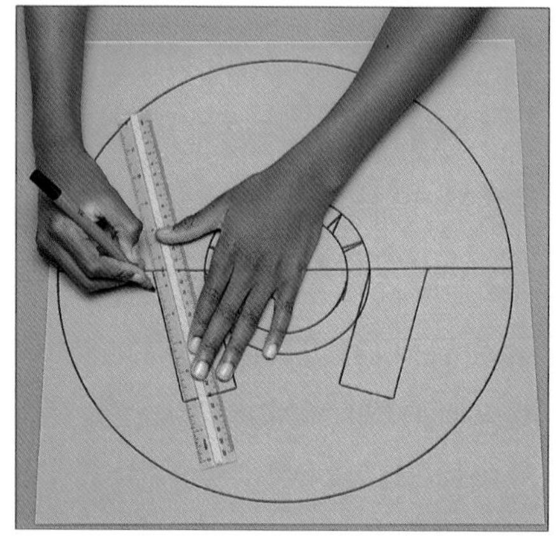

2 Draw a line across the centre of the three circles using a ruler and felt-tipped pen. Draw lines for tabs in the middle semicircle. Add two flaps either side as shown above.

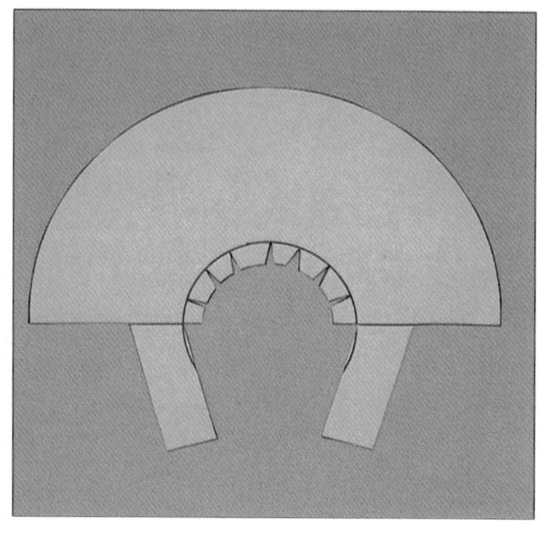

3 Cut out the neck protector piece completely to make the shape shown above. Make sure that you cut carefully around the flaps and along the lines between the tabs.

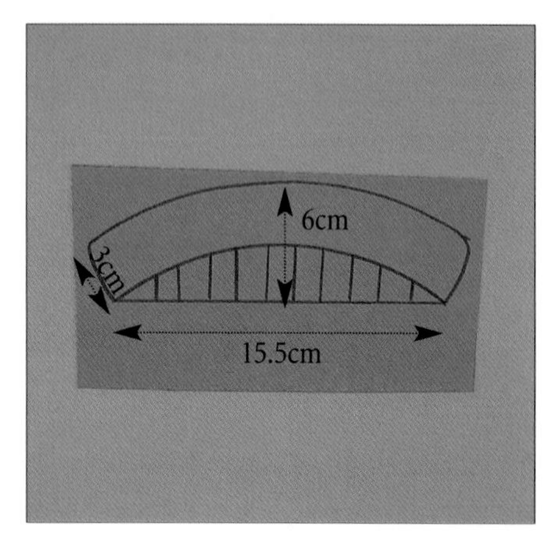

4 Draw the peak of the helmet on to another piece of card, using the measurements on the template above. Cut out the peak. Then blow up a balloon to the size of your head.

5 Cover the balloon with petroleum jelly. Tear newspaper into strips and add three layers of papier mâché (with two parts PVA glue to one part water) on the top and sides of the balloon.

6 When the papier mâché is dry, pop the balloon and trim the edges of the papier mâché cast. Ask a friend to make a mark with a pencil on either side of the helmet by your head.

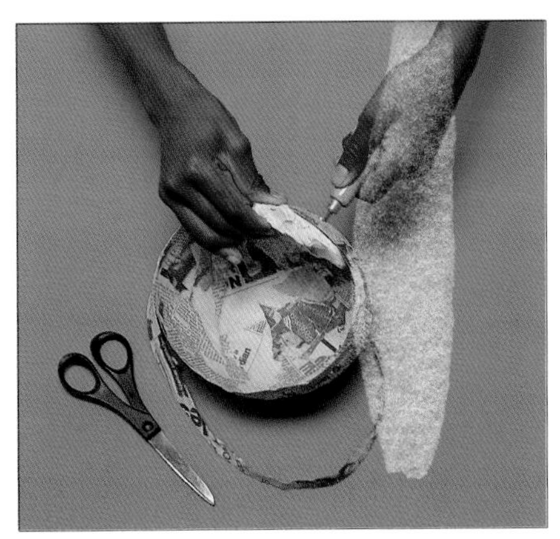

7 Place a piece of self-hardening clay under the pencil marks. Make two holes – one above and one below each pencil mark – with a bradawl. Repeat on the other side of the helmet.

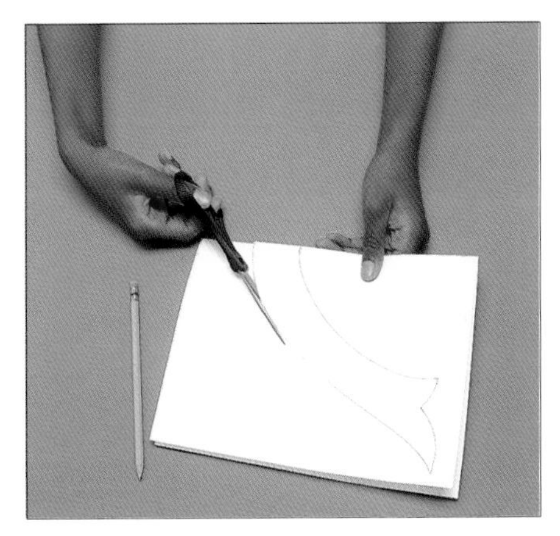

8 Fold a piece of A4 paper in half and draw a horn shape on to it using the design shown above as a guide. Cut out the shape so that you have an identical pair of horns.

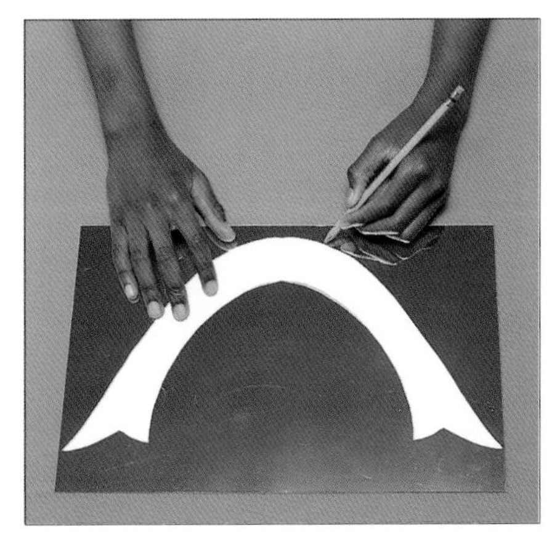

9 Take a piece of A4 gold card. Using the paper horns you have drawn as a template, draw the shape on to the gold card. Carefully cut the horns out of the card.

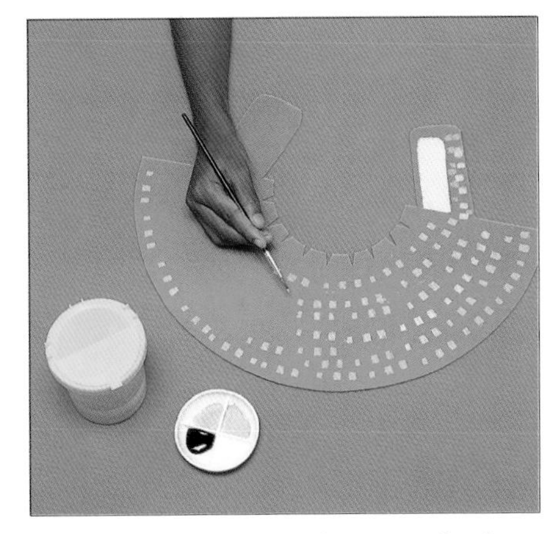

10 Paint a weave design on both sides of the neck protector and a cream block on each flap as shown above. Paint your papier mâché helmet brown. Leave the paint to dry.

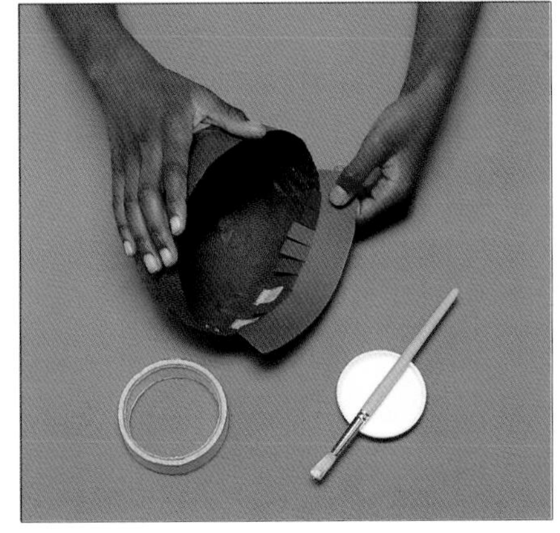

11 Cut and bend back the tabs on the peak of the helmet. Making sure the peak is at the front, glue the tabs to the inside as shown above. Secure the tabs with masking tape.

12 Now bend back the front flaps and the tabs of the neck protector and glue them to the helmet as shown above. Leave the helmet to dry completely.

13 Glue the gold card horns to the front of the helmet as shown above. Secure the horns with split pins. Use more split pins to decorate the ear flaps.

14 To wear your helmet, thread a piece of cord through one of the holes in the side of the helmet and tie a knot in the end. Thread the other end of the cord through the second hole. Repeat on the other side. Samurai helmets were often decorated with lacquered wood or metal crests mounted on the top of the helmet.

Viking shield

Norse warriors wore their own clothes and brought their own equipment to battle. Most wore caps of tough leather. Where metal helmets were worn, these were usually conical, and they sometimes had a bar to protect the nose. Viking raiders wore their everyday tunics and breeches and cloaks to keep out the cold. A rich Viking jarl (chieftain) might have a *brynja,* which was a shirt made up of interlinking rings of iron. Vikings also carried spears of various weights, longbows, deadly arrows and long-shafted battle axes on board the longship. The most prized weapon of all was the Viking sword. The blades of the swords were either made by Scandinavian blacksmiths or imported from Germany. A heavy shield, about 1m across, was made of wooden planks. It had an iron boss (central knob) and a rim of iron or leather.

YOU WILL NEED

Pair of compasses, pencil, card, string, scissors, red and gold paints, paintbrush, water pot, paper party bowl, newspaper, masking tape, PVA glue and glue brush, aluminium foil, brass split pins, craft knife, strip of wood, bias binding.

◂ Mass attack
Viking raiders disembark from their longships and race into action armed with their single-headed war axes. The Vikings used various axes for hacking the enemy at close range or for throwing from a distance. These iron-bladed weapons were often elaborately decorated.

1 Use the compasses to draw a small circle in the centre of a large piece of card. Then use a length of string tied to a pencil to draw a big circle for the shield as shown above.

2 Cut out the large circle. Then draw on a big, bold design such as the one shown in this project. Paint the shield with red and gold paint. Let the paint dry completely.

3 Use an upside down paper party bowl for the shield's central boss, or knob. Scrunch up some newspaper into a flattened ball and use masking tape to fix it to the top of the bowl.

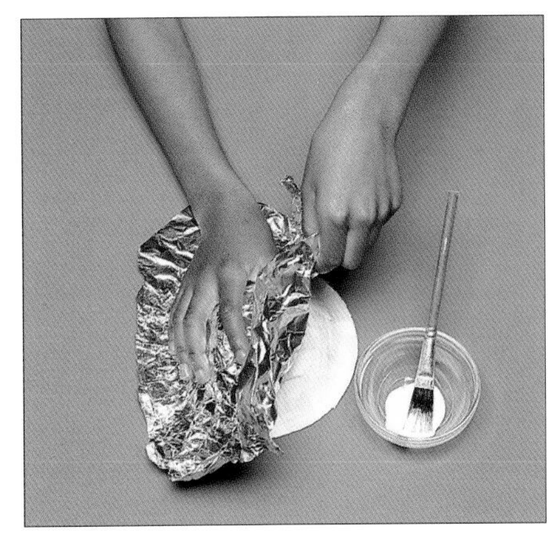

4 Spread PVA glue over the bowl and then cover it with aluminium foil. In Viking times, an iron boss would have strengthened the shield and protected the warrior's hand.

5 Glue the boss to the centre of your shield. Secure the boss with brass split pins punched through its edge and through the card of the shield.

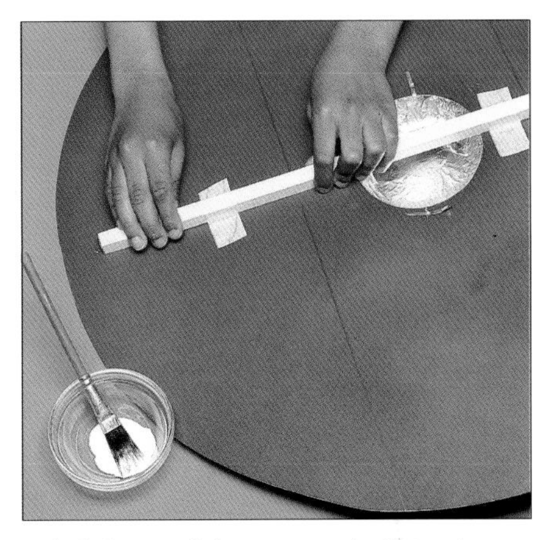

6 Ask an adult to cut a hole in the back of the shield where the boss is. Glue the strip of wood to the back of the shield and secure with strips of tape as shown above.

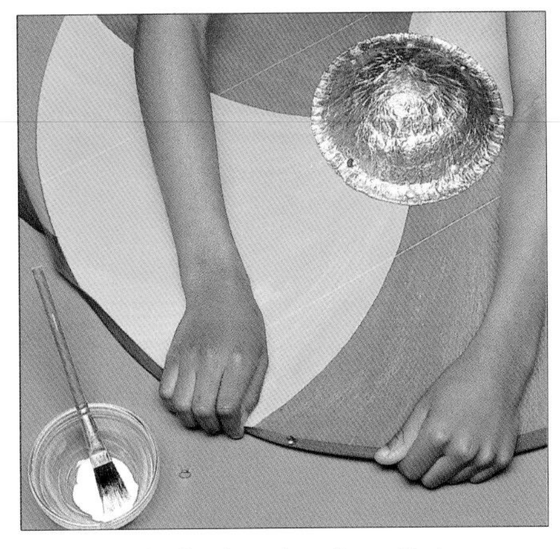

7 Attach the bias binding all the way around the rim of the shield using some brass split pins or small dabs of glue. Your shield is now ready for use in a Viking battle!

Give your shield its own Viking-style name, such as 'Fist of Thor' or 'Swordbreaker'.

Knight's helmet

A helmet protected the eyes and head of a soldier in battle. A flat-topped helmet was introduced in the 1100s, but it did not deflect blows as well as a rounded helmet. The basinet helmet of the 1300s had a moveable visor over the face. The introduction of hinges and pivots in the 1400s meant that a shaped helmet could be put on over the head and then closed to fit securely. From the 1500s, lighter, open helmets were worn. These were more comfortable, and soldiers could move around freely in battle.

YOU WILL NEED

Pencil, ruler, two large sheets of silver card, craft knife, cutting board, one large sheet of gold card, scissors, stapler and staples, PVA glue and glue brush, masking tape, pair of compasses, brass split pins.

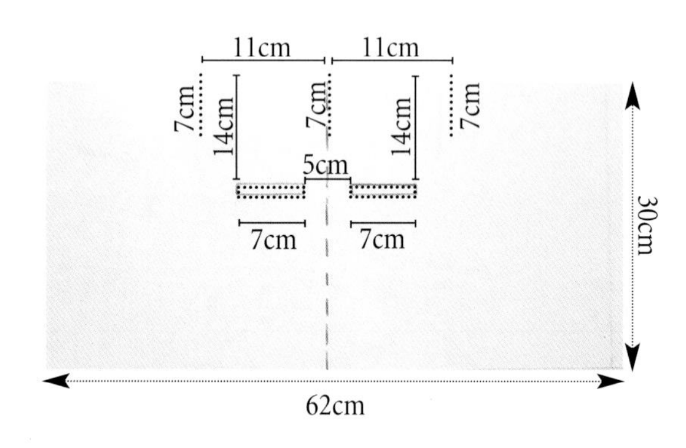

1 Using a pencil and the picture above as your guide, draw the template for your knight's helmet on to one large sheet of silver card. Measure and mark all the dotted lines as shown.

2 Use a craft knife, ruler and cutting board to cut out the eye slits. Cut a 62 x 4cm strip of gold card. Place it beneath the slits and draw the slits on the gold card. Cut them out.

3 Cut along the three 7cm dotted lines on the silver card template. Fold the card inwards as shown above to make the helmet curve. Staple the top of each overlapping section.

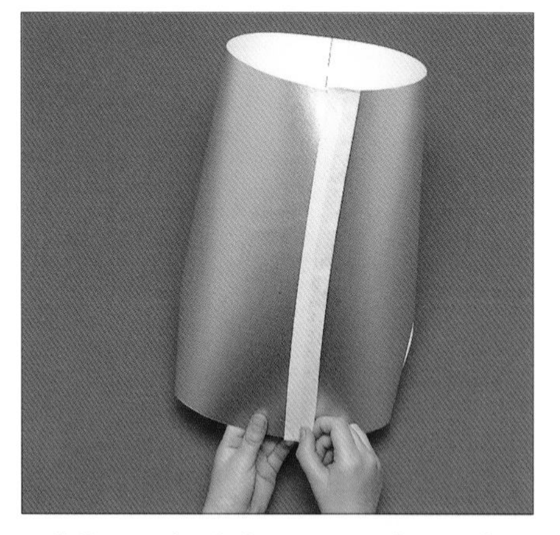

4 Curve the helmet into a long tube shape as shown. Glue and staple the tube together at the top and bottom. Secure the join with masking tape until the glue dries.

5 Set the compasses to 10cm and draw a circle (diameter 20cm) on the remaining silver card. Then set the compasses to 9cm and draw an inner circle with a diameter of 18cm.

6 Cut around the larger circle. Make cuts at 4cm intervals to the line of the inner circle. Bend them inwards and overlap. Fix tape on the back of the silver card to hold them in place.

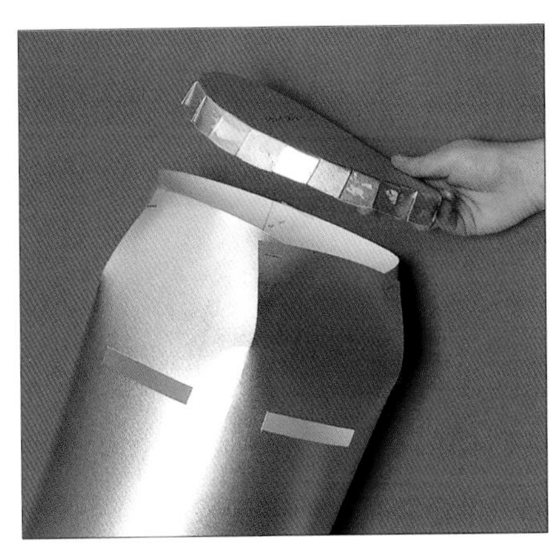

7 Put spots of glue on the outside top rim of the helmet. Hold the body of the helmet with one hand and carefully glue the top of the helmet on to the body with the other.

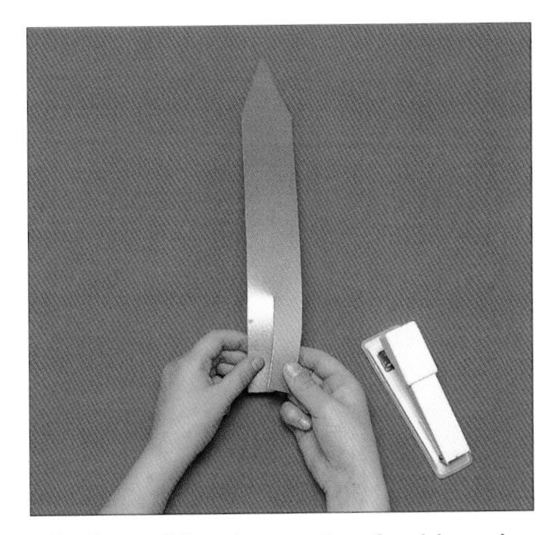

8 Cut a 30 x 4cm strip of gold card. Cut a point on one end of the strip. Cut a 7cm slit down the middle of the other end. Overlap the two flaps by about 1cm and staple.

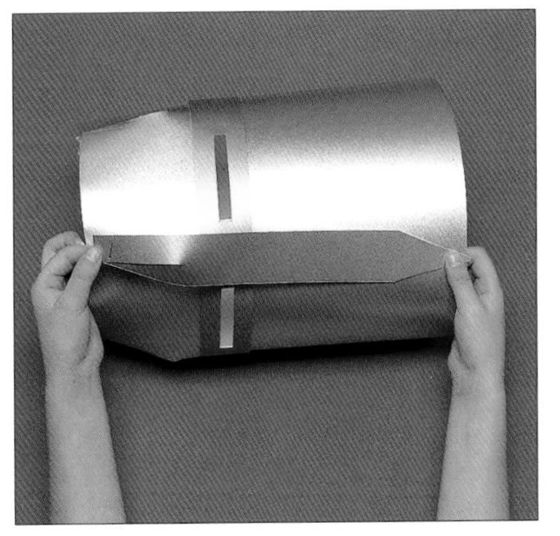

9 Staple the gold eye-slit strip into a circular band. Slip this over the helmet so that the eye slits match up. Glue it into position. Staple the nose piece in place between the eye slits.

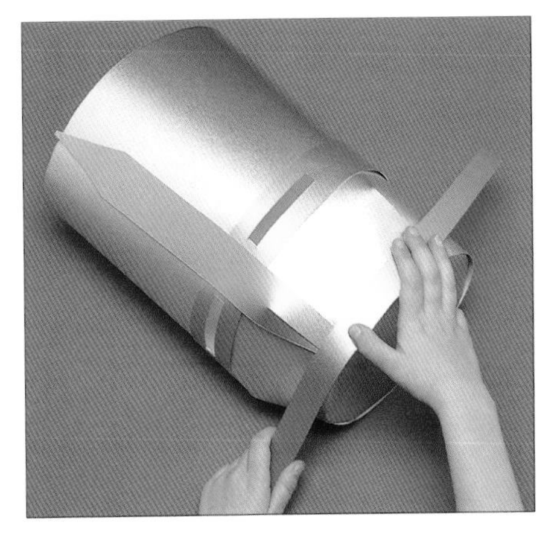

10 Cut a 62 x 2cm strip of gold card. Put spots of glue at intervals along the back of the card strip. Carefully stick the gold band around the top of the helmet.

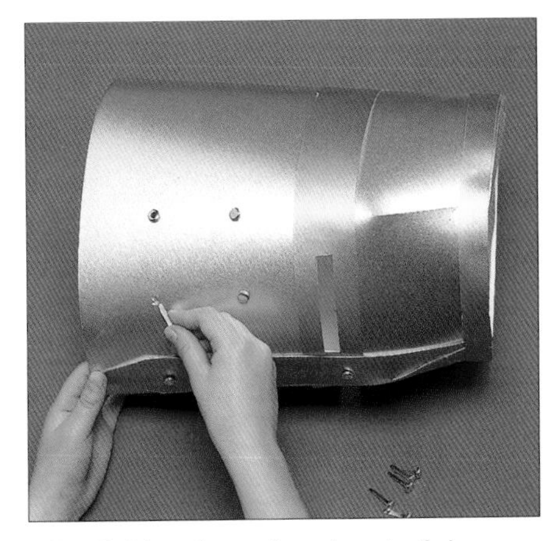

11 Use the pointed end of the compasses to pierce four holes on each 'cheek' of the helmet. Then make three holes along the nose piece. Push a brass split pin into each hole.

12 Split the pins and then cover the back of each one with strips of masking tape so that it does not scratch your face when you wear the helmet.

The Christian knights who fought in the Crusades wore helmets rather like the one you have made. Between 1095 and 1272, European knights fought Muslim countries for control of the Holy Land. The Crusaders wore a chainmail shirt, called a hauberk, with a cloth surcoat over the top. European armourers picked up some design ideas from their Muslim enemies, who were well-known for their skills in forging steel.

Medieval trebuchet

It took careful planning to mount a siege attack. Giant catapults played a vital role at the beginning of a siege. Their job was to weaken the castle defences before the foot soldiers moved in close. A deadly fire of boulders and flaming ammunition killed and maimed the fighters inside the castle walls. In the 1100s, powerful siege machines called trebuchets were developed to launch larger rocks over the castle walls. Decaying animals were also thrown over in the hope of spreading disease among the people inside.

YOU WILL NEED

Card, pencil, ruler, craft knife, cutting board, two 28cm and two 16cm strips of balsa, wood glue, pair of compasses, 32cm and 22cm length balsa dowelling, two 20 x 3.5 x 0.5cm pieces of balsa, scissors, four 25cm lengths square balsa dowelling, string, self-hardening clay, matchbox, acrylic paints, paintbrush, water pot.

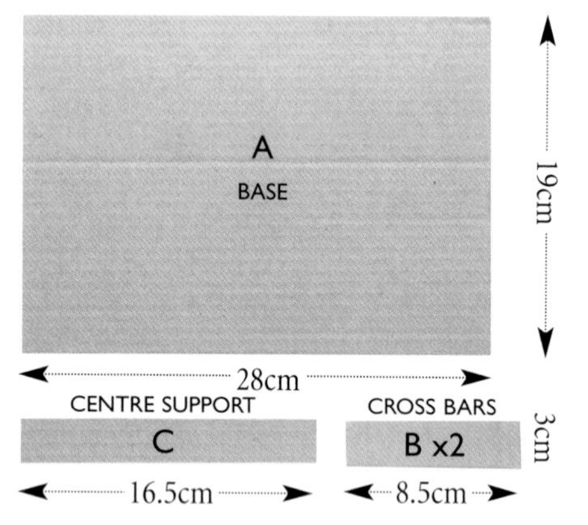

Copy the templates shown in the picture above on to a piece of thick card. Use a craft knife, cutting board and ruler to cut the pieces out.

1 Lay the base template A on to the work surface. Use wood glue to stick the two 28cm lengths and two 16cm lengths of balsa wood along each edge of the base section.

2 Use a sharp compass point to pierce a hole through the end of each of the 20cm lengths of balsa wood for side supports as shown in the picture above.

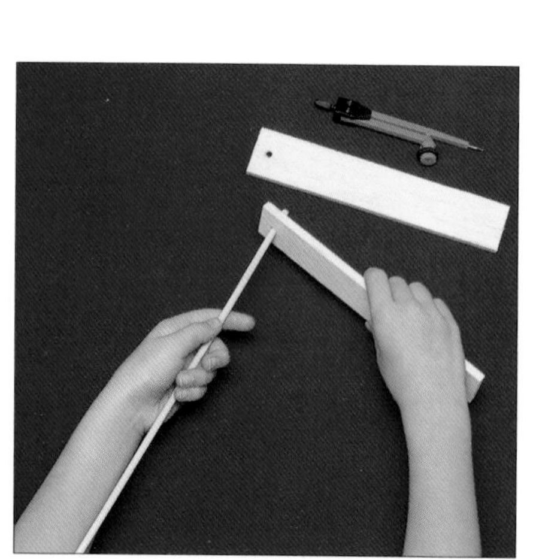

3 Use the sharp end of a pencil to make the hole a little bigger. Then push one of the pieces of balsa dowelling through each of the holes to make them the same diameter.

4 Use a pencil and ruler to draw two lines, 1cm from each end of the two crossbar sections B. Make a diagonal cut from the corners to the lines to make slanting edges.

5 Lay the 20cm balsa wood side supports on to the work surface. Glue the crossbars into position below the holes, about 3.5cm below the top of the side supports as shown above.

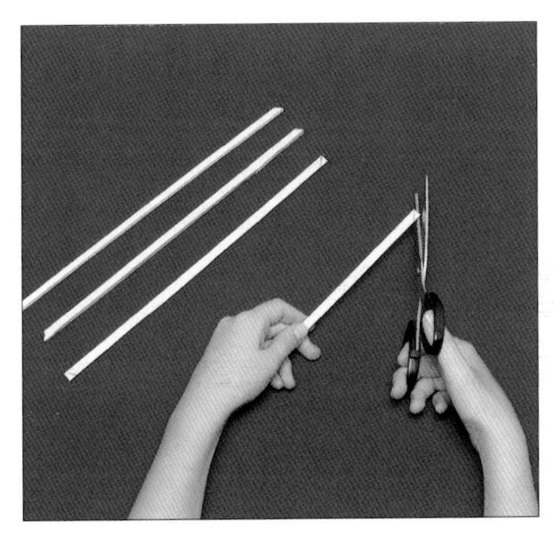

6 Place the four 25cm lengths of balsa wood dowelling on to the work surface. Ask an adult to help you cut both ends of the dowelling diagonally at an angle of 45 degrees.

7 Glue the supports mid-way along each long side of the base section. Glue the 25cm long balsa strips 2.5cm from the corners to form a triangle over the top of the support as shown.

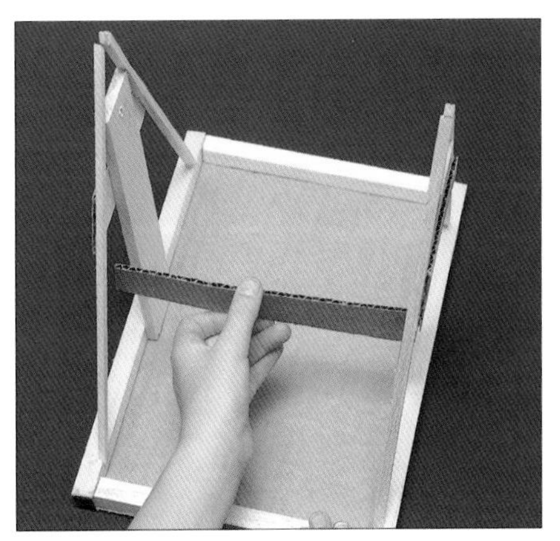

8 Glue along the ends on one side of the 16.5cm long centre support section. Stick it into place on the side supports, about 9cm from the base, as shown above.

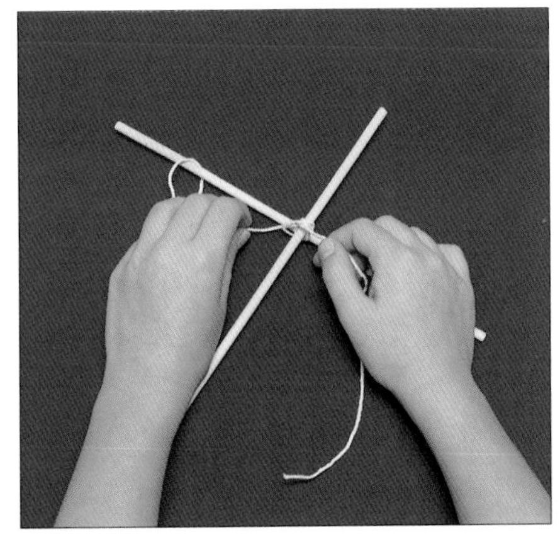

9 Make a 'T' shape with the 32cm and 22cm lengths of round dowelling with the shorter cross piece about 9cm from the top. Bind the pieces together tightly with string.

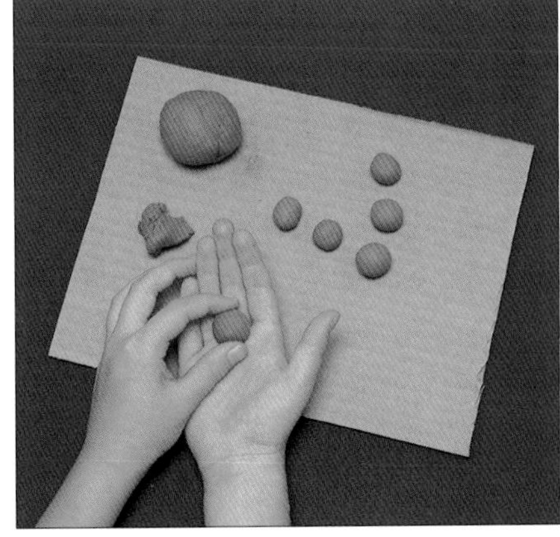

10 Roll some small pieces of clay in the palm of your hands. Mould one big ball about 5cm in diameter and some smaller balls. Leave the clay balls to one side to dry.

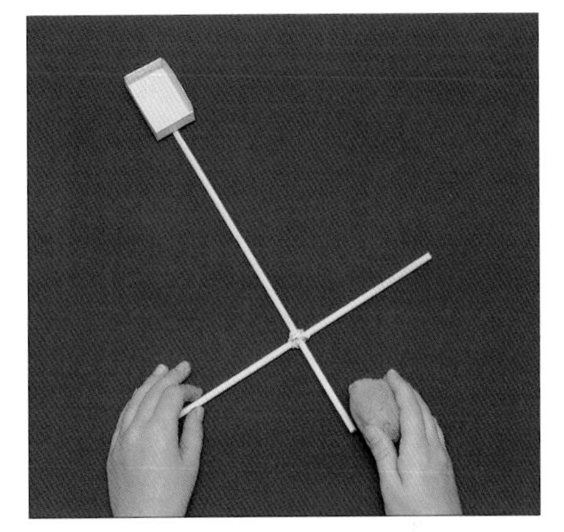

11 Glue the back of the inside of a matchbox. Stick this to the bottom of the long arm of the cross piece. Stick the big clay ball on to the other end.

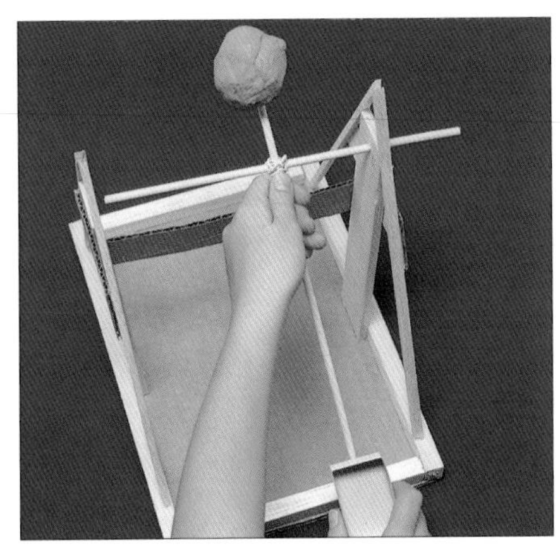

12 Fit the arms of the cross piece into the holes in the balsa wood side supports so that the matchbox is at the bottom. Finally, paint the model with acrylic paints.

Put some clay balls into the matchbox and raise the big ball. Drop it to let the missiles fly! The clay missiles fired from your trebuchet are unlikely to do much damage. However, with its long weighted arm and open support frame, the model trebuchet operates in much the same way as the real thing. The word *trebuchet* comes from a French word for a similar device that was used for shooting birds.

Cut-throat cutlass

The swords carried by pirates have varied greatly over the ages. Ancient Greek pirates fought with a 60cm-long, leaf-shaped blade or with a curved cut-and-thrust blade called a kopis. Their Roman enemies fought with a short sword called a gladius. Viking swords were long and double-edged for heavy slashing. The rapier, introduced in the 1500s, was a light sword with a deadly, pointed blade, but it was too long and delicate for close-range fighting on board ship. The cutlass was the ideal weapon for that.

▲ **Pirate sword**
The most common and useful pirate weapon was probably the cutlass, used from the 1600s onwards.

YOU WILL NEED

Two pieces of stiff card measuring 45 x 5cm, pencil, scissors, PVA glue and glue brush, newspaper, masking tape, one piece of stiff card (30 x 10cm), one cup of flour, half a cup of water, mixing bowl, spoon, sandpaper, brown and silver acrylic paint, two paintbrushes, water pot, black felt-tipped pen, ruler, wood varnish.

1 Take one piece of the stiff card measuring 45 x 5cm. Carefully pencil in an outline of a cutlass blade and hilt (handle) on to the piece of card as shown above.

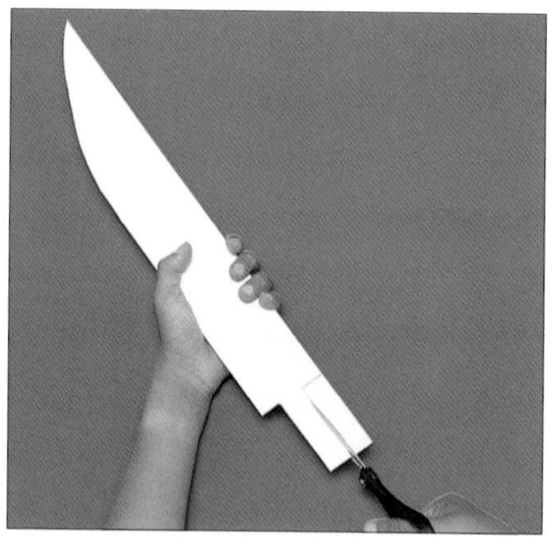

2 Use a pair of scissors to cut the shape out. Use this as a template to lay on the second piece of card. Draw around the template and then cut out a second cutlass shape.

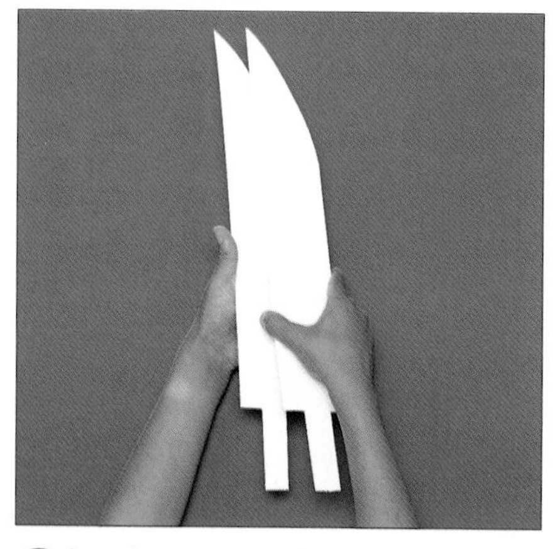

3 Lay the two matching sections of the cutlass on top of each other as shown above. Glue them together. The double thickness gives the finished cutlass extra strength.

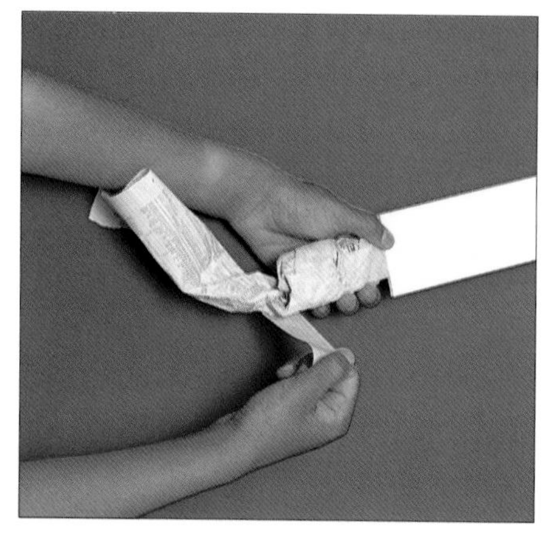

4 Twist a piece of newspaper into thick strips to wind around the hilt. The newspaper should be thick enough to make a comfortable handgrip. Bind the newspaper with masking tape.

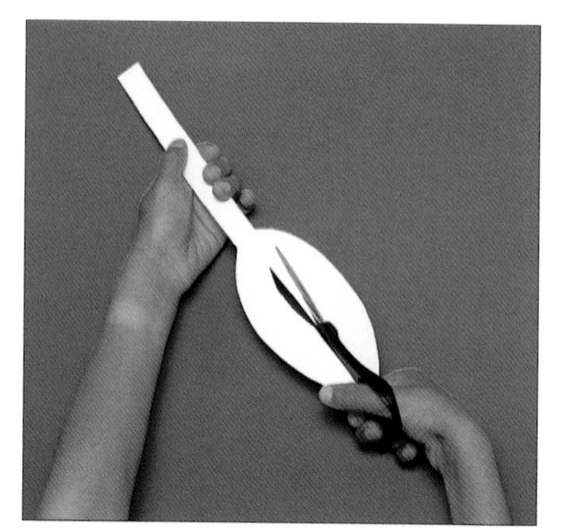

5 Draw the shape of a cutlass handle on to the stiff piece of 30 x 10cm card and cut it out. Make a cut down the middle of the wide end to about 2.5cm short of the stem as shown.

6 Tape the narrow stem of the handle to the end of the cutlass hilt. Bend the rest of the handle around to slot over the curved edge of the blade as shown above.

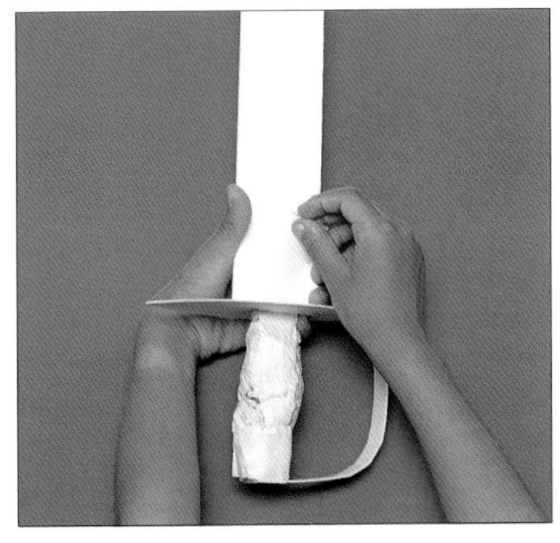

7 Make sure the oval lies flat against the hilt of the cutlass to form the hand guard. Use masking tape to seal the slit and to secure the handle of the cutlass to the blade.

8 Pour the flour into a mixing bowl and slowly add the water, a spoon at a time, mixing as you go. The mixture should form a smooth, thick paste similar to pancake batter.

9 Tear newspaper into short strips and coat these with the paste. Cover the cutlass with three layers of papier mâché. Leave the cutlass in a warm place for several hours.

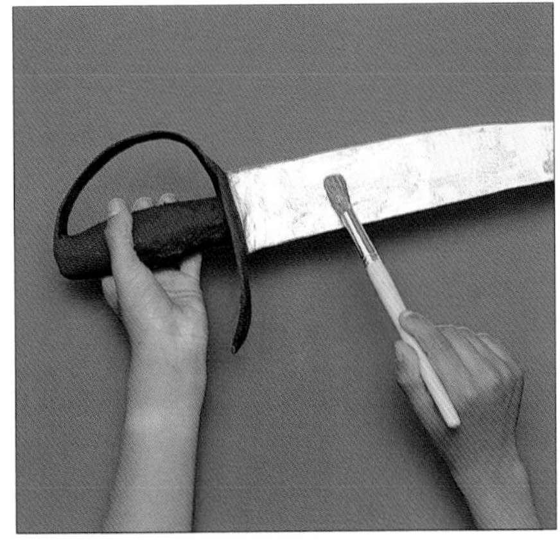

10 When the cutlass is dry, smooth it down using sandpaper. Paint the cutlass with acrylic paint as shown. Allow the first coat to dry thoroughly and then apply another coat of paint.

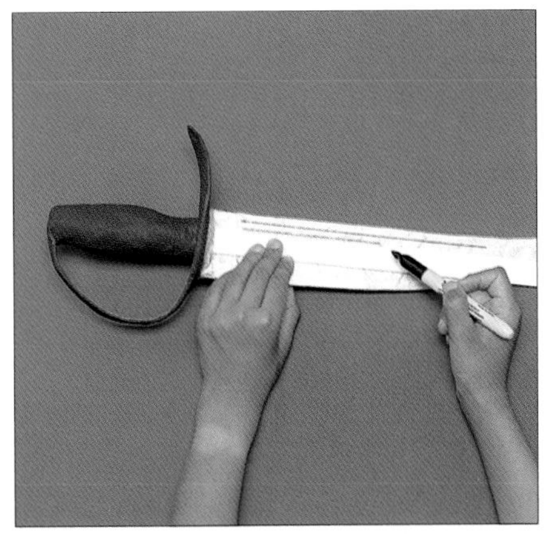

11 When the second coat of paint is completely dry, use a black felt-tipped pen and ruler to add fine details on the blade of the cutlass as shown above.

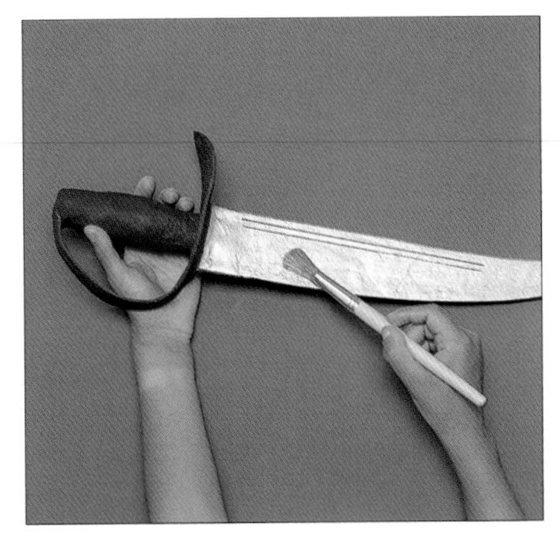

12 Finally, use a clean paintbrush to apply a coat of wood varnish to the blade and hilt. This will toughen the cutlass as well as giving it a menacing glint.

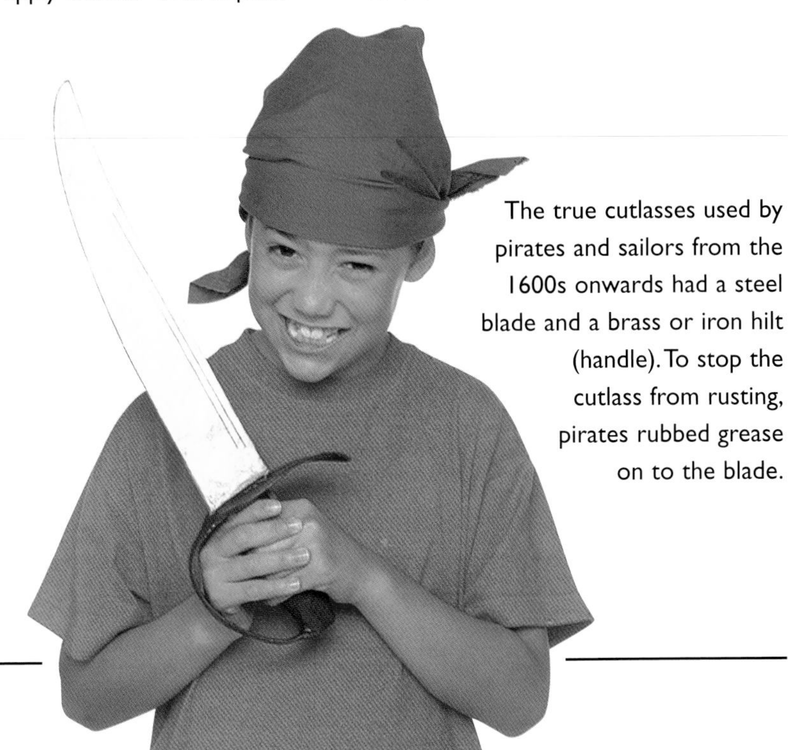

The true cutlasses used by pirates and sailors from the 1600s onwards had a steel blade and a brass or iron hilt (handle). To stop the cutlass from rusting, pirates rubbed grease on to the blade.

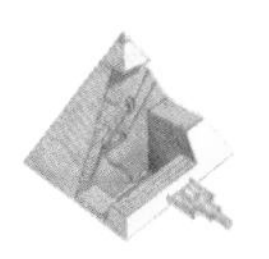

Glossary

A

ancestor A member of the same family who died long ago.

Anno Domini (AD) A system used to calculate dates after the supposed year of Jesus Christ's birth. Anno Domini dates in this book are prefixed AD up to the year 1000, for example, AD521. After 1000 no prefixes are used.

archaeologist Someone who studies ancient ruins and artefacts to learn about the past.

archaeology The scientific study of the past, which involves looking at the remains of ancient civilizations.

Arctic A vast, frozen area surrounding the North Pole.

arithmetic Any calculation that involves the use of numbers.

armour A suit worn by people or horses to protect them against injury during battle.

Assyrian An inhabitant of the Assyrian Empire. From 1530-612BC, Assyria stretched from east of the Mediterranean Sea to Iran, and from the Persian Gulf to eastern Turkey.

astrolabe A device invented by the Arabs, which consisted of a flat disc with a rod that could be pointed to the stars. Astrolabes helped sailors to navigate when travelling on water.

astrology The belief that stars, planets and other heavenly bodies shape the lives of people on Earth.

astronomy The scientific study of stars, planets and other heavenly bodies. In ancient times, astronomy was the same as astrology.

auxiliaries Foreign troops that help and support another nation that is engaged in war.

Aztecs Mesoamerican people who lived in northern and central Mexico. The Aztecs were at their most powerful between the period of 1350 and 1520.

B

barter An exchange of goods that does not involve money.

Before Christ (BC) A system that is used to calculate dates before the supposed year of Jesus Christ's birth. Dates are calculated in reverse order. For example, 2000BC is longer ago than 200BC.

brahmin A Hindu who belongs to the highest of four social classes.

Bronze Age A period in history, between 3000 and 1000BC, when tools and weapons were made from bronze.

Buddhism World religion founded in ancient India by the Buddha in the 6th century BC.

C

canal An artificial channel or waterway, usually constructed to allow boats to carry goods from one place to another but sometimes built to improve drainage or irrigation of a particular area of land.

caste One of four social classes that divides the followers of the Hindu religion.

catapult A large wooden structure used to fire stones and iron bolts at the enemy during medieval sieges.

cavalry Soldiers on horseback.

Celt A member of one of the ancient peoples that inhabited most parts of Europe from around 750BC to AD1000.

chainmail Flexible armour that is worn on the body, consisting of small rings of metal linked to form a fine mesh.

chariot A lightweight, horse-drawn cart. Chariots were used in warfare and for sport.

circa (*c.*) A symbol used to mean 'approximately,' when the exact date of an event is not known e.g. *c.* 1000BC.

citizen A Roman term used to describe a free person with the right to vote.

civilization A society that makes advances in arts, sciences, law, technology and government.

colonies Communities or groups of people who settle in another land but keep links with their own country.

coracle A small boat made of leather tightly stretched over a wooden frame.

crossbow A mechanical bow that fires small arrows called bolts.

cuirass Armour that protects the upper part of the body.

D

daimyo A nobleman or warlord from ancient Japan.

decimal system A system of measurement with units that are related to each other by multiples of 10.

dictator A ruler with complete and unrestricted power.

dowel A thin cylindrical length of wood. Dowelling is available from hardware stores.

domesticated A word used to describe animals that have been tamed and are kept as pets or farm animals. For example, cats and dogs as pets and sheep on a farm.

dynasty A successive period of rule by generations of the same family.

E

empire A group of lands ruled or governed by a single nation.

F

flood An overflow of water from rivers, lakes or the sea on to the dry land.

G

garrison A fort or similar place that is guarded by a group of soldiers. The word garrison can also refer to the group of soldiers themselves.

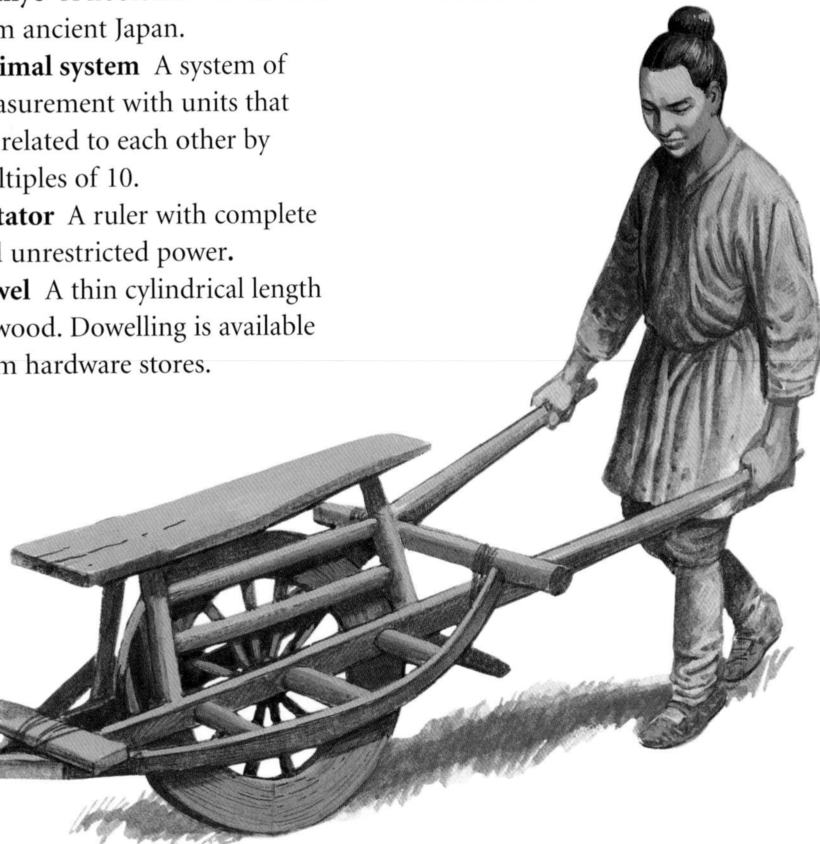

geisha A Japanese woman who entertains men with song and dances.
gladiator A professional fighter, a slave or a criminal in ancient Rome, who fought to the death in arenas for the public.
greaves Armour that is worn to protect the shins.
groma An instrument used by Roman surveyors to measure right angles and to make sure roads were straight.

H
hoplites Greek fighting force made up of middle-class men. Their armour and weaponry was of the highest standard.
husky An Inuit dog with a thick coat and curled tail used as a sledge-dog in the Arctic.

I
Inca A member of an indigenous South American civilization living in Peru before the Spanish conquest.
Inuit The native people of the Arctic and regions of Greenland, Alaska and Canada.
invent To be the first person to make or use something. For example, a machine, game, method, etc.
irrigation Using channels dug into the earth to bring water to dry land so that crops can grow.

J
Junk A far Eastern, flat-bottomed square sailed boat.

K
kayak A one-person Inuit canoe powered by a double-bladed paddle. The wooden or bone frame is covered with sealskin.

L
legion The main unit of the Roman army made up only of Roman citizens.

M
Maya An ancient civilization native to Mesoamerica.
medieval A term describing people, events and objects from a period in history known as the Middle Ages.
merchant Someone whose job it is to sell goods.
Mesopotamia An ancient name for the fertile region between the Tigris and Euphrates rivers in the Middle East. This area is now occupied by Iraq.

N
Native Americans The indigenous peoples of the Americas.
nomads A group of people who roam from place to place in search of food or better land, or to follow herds.

O
oppidum A Latin word that means town.

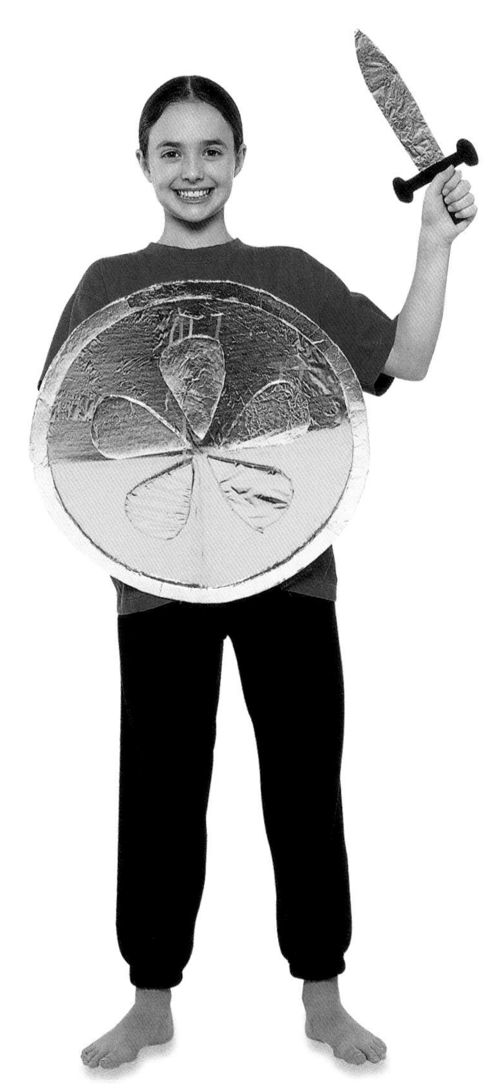

sampan A small Oriental boat that has no engine and is propelled by oars.
samurai Members of the Japanese warrior class. Samurai were highly trained and followed a strict code of honourable behaviour.
settlement A recently settled community or colony.
shogun A Japanese army commander. Shoguns ruled Japan from 1185-1868.
siege A long-lasting attack to capture a fortified place or city by surrounding it and cutting off all supplies.
society All the classes of people living in a particular community or country.
Stone Age The first period in human history in which people made their tools and weapons out of stone.

T
template A piece of card cut in a particular design and used as a pattern when cutting out material. You can use a photocopier to enlarge the templates in this book. Alternatively, copy the templates on to a piece of paper, using a ruler to make sure the size follows the measurements given in the book.
temple A building used for worship or other spiritual rituals.
territory The land under control of a ruler, government or state.
trade The process of buying and selling.

V
Viking One of the Scandinavian peoples who lived by carrying out sea raids in the early Middle Ages. They settled in various parts of Europe.

P
pirate Someone who attacks and robs ships at sea.

Q
quipu Knotted, coloured cords tied together and used by the Incas to record information.

R
ramparts The defensive parapets that are built on the top of castle walls.
rapier A long, thin sword.
regent Someone who rules a country on behalf of another person.

S
Saami The ancient people of Lapland in Scandinavia.

Index